That
presentation
sensation

FINANCIAL TIMES
Prentice Hall

In an increasingly competitive world, it is quality
of thinking that gives an edge – an idea that opens new
doors, a technique that solves a problem, or an insight
that simply helps make sense of it all.

We work with leading authors in the fields of
management and finance to bring cutting-edge thinking
and best learning practice to a global market.

Under a range of leading imprints, including
Financial Times Prentice Hall, we create world-class
print publications and electronic products giving readers
knowledge and understanding which can then be
applied, whether studying or at work.

To find out more about our business and professional
products, you can visit us at www.business-minds.com

For other Pearson Education publications, visit
www.pearsoned-ema.com

Pearson
Education

That presentation sensation

LET THE BEST IN THE BUSINESS SHOW YOU
HOW TO BE GOOD, BE PASSIONATE,
BE UNFORGETTABLE

Martin Conradi and Richard Hall

FINANCIAL TIMES
Prentice Hall

an imprint of Pearson Education

London • New York • San Francisco • Toronto • Sydney • Tokyo • Singapore • Hong Kong
Cape Town • Madrid • Paris • Milan • Munich • Amsterdam

PEARSON EDUCATION LIMITED

Head Office:
Edinburgh Gate
Harlow
CM20 2JE
Tel: +44 (0)1279 623623
Fax: +44 (0)1279 431059

London Office:
128 Long Acre
London WC2E 9AN
Tel: +44 (0)20 7447 2000
Fax: +44 (0)20 7240 5771
Website: www.business-minds.com

First published in Great Britain in 2001

© Pearson Education Limited 2001

The right of Martin Conradi and Richard Hall to be identified as authors of this work has been
asserted by them in accordance with the Copyright, Designs and Patents Act 1988.

ISBN 0 273 65474 8

British Library Cataloguing-in-Publication Data

A CIP catalogue record for this book can be obtained from the British Library

10 9 8 7 6 5 4 3 2 1

Design by Claire Brodmann Book Designs, Lichfield, Staffs
Typeset by Northern Phototypesetting Co. Ltd, Bolton
Printed and bound in Great Britain by Biddles Ltd, Guildford & King's Lynn

The Publishers' policy is to use paper manufactured from sustainable forests.

CONTENTS

ACKNOWLEDGMENTS x
INTRODUCTION xii

part one
PRESENTATIONS AS A KEY PART OF EVERYDAY LIFE *1*

chapter one
'Once more unto the breach dear friends ...'
Great speakers and how they move an audience *3*

chapter two
A classic presentation
A guide to current malpractice *16*

chapter three
Telling tales
Breaking down barriers—the importance of stories *32*

chapter four
The practice of presentation
Presentations are too important to busk *39*

INSPIRERS, PERSPIRERS, ASPIRERS *part one*
Interviews with master presenters *45*

part two
PRESENTATIONS THAT INSPIRE OR CONFUSE OR SIMPLY SELL *77*

chapter five
'I'm your boss – now what was it you wanted to tell me?'
Finding a common language *79*

chapter six
'I'm your boss – trust me, follow me, respect me'
Delivering the message *82*

chapter seven

The shining white teeth of the super salesman

The sales pitch   91

chapter eight

The final analysis

Justifying your performance   105

INSPIRERS, PERSPIRERS, ASPIRERS *part two*

Interviews with master presenters   115

part three

PROPS, AIDS AND ZIMMER FRAMES

– the stuff that makes presentations work or fail   147

PRESENTATION MASTERS   *after page 144*

chapter nine

The use and abuse of visual aids

Visual aids and why they matter   149

chapter ten

Sliding with confidence

Making slides work for you   156

chapter eleven

Fear of flying

Honing the cutting edge   169

chapter twelve

Getting it right on the night

Making it all work on stage   180

chapter thirteen

Snatching triumph from the jaws of disaster

When it all goes wrong   193

chapter fourteen
Taming the technicians
> *Conferences and how to survive them*   *211*

chapter fifteen
Presenting into the future
> *Where is all this technology taking us?*   *215*

INSPIRERS, PERSPIRERS, ASPIRERS *part three*
> *Interviews with master presenters*   *223*

part four
THE WORLD OF PRESENTATIONS *249*

chapter sixteen
The Tower of Babel
> *Presenting to multinational audiences*   *251*

chapter seventeen
Welcome to presentation city
> *Global presentations in today's world*   *258*

**OH MY AMERICA, MY NEW FOUND LAND
(OR WHY WE FIND AMERICAN PRESENTATIONS SEXY)**
> *Interviews with master presenters*   *261*

part five
CONCLUSIONS, CONFUSIONS AND CURTAIN CALLS *289*

chapter eighteen
And finally ...   *291*

CONTRIBUTORS

MARJORIE SCARDINO—*Pearson*

MIKE GRABINER—*formerly of Energis*

LUCY PARKER—*Trinity*

HOWARD COATES—*Makinson Cowell*

ANTHONY CARLISLE—*Citigate Dewe Rogerson*

ALAN PARKER—*Brunswick*

JOHN BEAUMONT—*Energis Squared*

ROGER MAVITY—*boxclever*

LEON KREITZMAN—*author and guru*

DAVID ABBOTT—*formerly of Abbott Mead Vickers/BBDO*

DAVID HESLOP—*Mazda Cars*

DIANNE THOMPSON—*Camelot*

MIKE KIRSCH—*Norwich Union Life*

CHRIS PINNINGTON—*Euro RSCG Wnek Gosper*

LUCAS VAN PRAAG—*Goldman Sachs*

SIMON SKELDON—*Taylor Nelson Sofres*

DR NEVILLE BAIN—*Consignia*

MICHAEL ULLMANN—*INSEAD*

MARCUS ALEXANDER—*London Business School*

COLIN PRESCOT—*Flying Pictures*

PAUL BARRATT—*Gaskell*

CHRIS MILBURN—*Centrica*

2 SENIOR CIVIL SERVANTS—*anonymous*

JILL KNIGHT—*Baroness and politician*

KAIZO MANAGEMENT TEAM

SIMON WALKER—*Communications Secretary for HM the Queen*

JOHN TRIGGLE, CHARLES ROSNER—*HTRP*
NIGEL CLARE—*formerly of Heinz*
TERESA CEBALLOS—*Heinz*
MARC WOLFF—*pilot*

Interviews with Olivier Fleurot (Financial Times) *and David Reed*
(Whitbread) are included in Chapter Six.

ACKNOWLEDGEMENTS

To all our contributors who showed such wit, wisdom, interest and insight.

To KATE HALL and BARBARA GOWLAND for their patience, encouragement and diplomacy.

To NICKI BARTLEY who could read, almost, Richard's writing.

To our colleagues at Showcase Presentations who kept the show on the road so ably while we wrote and talked and argued (and to SANDRA LEE in particular).

To our many clients over the years who have trusted us and come back for more.

And to all presenters everywhere who invariably run out of time and resources and so make this such a perennially lively and fascinating business with so many problems and rather fewer answers.

RICHARD HALL is Chairman of Showcase Presentations, Flying Pictures, Argyll Communications, Shaftesbury Homes and Arethusa, and senior partner of Hall, Triggle, Rosner and Parker.

MARTIN CONRADI pioneered the use of computers in business presentations back in the early 1980s. He is Managing Director of Showcase Presentations.

We had **snakes** in *Raiders of the Lost Ark* and
bugs in *Indiana Jones and The Temple of Doom*.
But supposedly
man's greatest fear is
public speaking.
That'll be in our next picture.

Steven Speilberg

There is **serious danger** in
being thought a **brilliant presenter**

Gordon Owen, Chairman, Energis Plc

Bad presentation is **tantamount
to fraud**

Financial Times

"I want to see the whites of their eyes."

These words were from a City analyst, discussing presentations by senior executives. Why bother with presentations, we had asked. Why go out early on a wet, cold Monday morning when they will happily send you the presentation on disk, e-mail you the script, talk to you on the phone or web-cast it to your desk? Why are live presentations so important?

The whites of their eyes.

It is not just substance; style really matters.

It's not (just) what you say, it's the way that you say it.

❝Body language rules OK. Is the CEO simply nervous or is he being shifty? And if he's nervous, why is he? He's a CEO for goodness sake, being paid a modest fortune. He's no right to be nervous unless, of course, he's got something to hide. And look at his eyes. A dead giveaway. Blinking. Looking down at his notes. Glancing backwards at the screen. No eye contact at all. And now he's closed them altogether. Is he praying? Is he praying we'll swallow this codswallop hook, line and sinker?❞

None of this could happen to the recipient who couldn't get to the presentation and simply read the handout in the calm of his or her office, where everything has to be taken at face value.

No, it's the eyes that have it. They are the windows to the corporate soul.

The whole subject of presentations is one that evokes considerable interest from everyone in business today. And not just business. People in general recognize that a well-presented argument – be it in court, at a planning enquiry or even in church – has a better chance of being well received.

The importance of presentations today is enormous. Poor presenters get fired or at best don't get hired. It is the entry price for new CEOs that they are an excellent presenter.

And being excellent does not mean being a formulaic presenter who neither stutters nor blushes nor gabbles. It means someone capable of grabbing our attention.

From the many interviews with the great, the good and those destined to be very successful, two or three things have become clear.

It's absolutely about discovering your own voice.

Firstly, there are no consistent rules to being a presenter who excels. It's absolutely about discovering your own voice, your own way of talking, of using visual aids, of pacing yourself. So if you have got this far in the hope of finding some rote answers to your particular presentational problems, you may find this book disappointing, although (as you will discover) it's actually rather exciting.

Secondly, there are many different types of presentation. Just as no sane marketeer would dream of creating a communications campaign without a strategy, without understanding the target market and without some considerable thought and research, so no sane presenter ...

part one

PRESENTATIONS AS

A KEY PART OF EVERYDAY LIFE

chapter one
' Once more unto the breach dear friends …'   3

chapter two
A classic presentation   16

chapter three
Telling tales   32

chapter four
The practice of presentation   39

INSPIRERS, PERSPIRERS, ASPIRERS   45
Interviews with master presenters

John Beaumont	– *Energis Squared*
Roger Mavity	– *boxclever*
Leon Kreitzman	– *author and guru*
David Abbott	– *formerly of Abbott Mead Vickers/BBDO*
David Heslop	– *Mazda Cars*
Dianne Thompson	– *Camelot*

sure our Prime Minister would see himself thus cast – can blow it when they try the morale booster.

So what went wrong? Wrong audience, wrong message, most of all wrong medium. He wasn't really talking to the blue-rinsed viragos of Cheltenham. They were merely a conduit to 'us' – the electorate, and they had pretty well decided to give him the raspberry if he so much as strayed off a 'good afternoon it's nice to be here' message. They were out to get him. He was out to get to us and, quite simply, they ambushed him.

The lesson to all leaders is clear. Do your reconnaissance carefully. Speak to the audience you have, *not* the one you wish you had. And if you want to boost morale, understand exactly where the morale of the audience is before you press the boost button.

Speak to the audience you have, not the one you wish you had.

My scepticism about morale boosting presentations is based on my belief in the frailty of morale as a corporate concept. I'm often asked about companies I visit, how's morale? What does it really mean? Are people cheerful and motivated? Are they performing well as a team? Are they seeing through the corporate myth? Or quite simply are they 'on message'? Are they, from a management perspective, easy to manage, biddable to management directives?

And it is on morale boosting we focus in this chapter since nearly everyone we've spoken to confesses to the difficulties of 'turning on' and 'tuning in' an audience.

Every manager will have to give an adrenalin boost to those who work for them sometime or another. Our advice is to spare the rod of morale boosting for a few very well chosen moments.

For that first defining moment. Your first presentation to your top team or to your company when you're made Chief Executive.

For some occasion when you need a productivity boost and a real sense of focus. In the face of a takeover, for instance, or when you're on the acquisition trail.

And for when you're absolutely up against it, when disaster is staring you in the face and you haven't the faintest idea what to do except appeal to your employees' better natures.

The presentations people remember are the ones that precede success and there are three I want to consider. The first is Henry V before the Battle of Agincourt. Shakespeare might take it somewhat amiss to hear his crafted speech called a presentation. There's the play of course and the real history. Henry's troops decimated and in retreat, riddled with dysentery and up against France's finest and fittest. Not a chance. They all faced certain death and whether it happened quite like this or not is immaterial – we just have to believe it did. A young man's inspiring words, a pragmatic battle strategy, a rainstorm that reduced the charge of the French cavalry to a squelchy amble through thick mud, and French insanity (if only all our competitors would behave like that) pulled a triumphant rabbit of victory out of an extremely unpromising hat. Good presentation: lots of luck.

This was, of course, Henry's second great presentation in as many hours. His first, at Harfleur, is considered in more detail shortly.

The second is Abraham Lincoln's presentation at Gettysburg (oh all right, it was an address). Abe batted second and his predecessor, we're told, spoke for several hours. No one today can remember a word or even his predecessor's name. There's a sharp reminder that less can be more.

The third is George C. Scott's speech in *Patton*, the slightly untidy film about the eccentric but charismatic World War II general. Here we see the true art of presentation. Behind a huge American flag, head emerging first as he strides up a long flight of stairs, then torso, then the whole gloriously uniformed Patton, ivory handled revolvers and all. He even makes me want to fight. Anyone.

And of course the morale boosters I've cited succeeded. Those

But beware the morale-boosting presentation which is that alone and has no follow through.

whose morale is boosted will be in a temporary state of euphoria at best and in the days and weeks that follow they will expect you and your promises to become tangible.

The exception is the management guru. They invest you, the audience, with a heady stream of tips, prescriptions and anecdotes and after they've finished it's up to you, buster, to make of it what you will.

Anyone who's seen Rosabeth Moss Kanter or Tom Peters in action knows what I mean. Tom in particular struts the room working himself into a lather of loathing for big business. Take airlines, for example:

66If you want to become an airline pilot, they ask you three questions. One, can you see? Two, can you move your hands and legs? Actually these first two don't matter that much, it's the third question that's the clincher – are you a congenital liar?99

He rants and rails about airlines' failure to manage realities, let alone customer expectations. About 'we'll take off ladies and gentlemen in the next 15 minutes' always but always being barefacedly mendacious. The stand-up guru unleashes anecdote after anecdote to a laughing, squirming audience (especially squirming if they happen to work for British Airways) and then changes pace and focus.

66So what's this all mean?99

He flicks on his next slide which is long and learned and has *Harvard Business Review* at the bottom.

66Managing customer expectations so they sustain trust in a corporation and so their experience of a company always exceeds their expectation is the key to building and maintaining a customer-facing brand ...99

He reads it slowly, word by word, and glares at his audience, all of whom are by now writing careful notes.

66It's that simple and that fundamental.99

Now hang on Tom, you've lulled me into a false sense of hysteria and then you've nailed me with a cliché which because of its academic provenance is supposedly irrefutable. Yet the experience is curiously uplifting.

It's an old technique that really works – hard man, soft man, ever changing. Tony O'Reilly uses it and his Irish lilt helps his cause. This is from a Marketing Society dinner many years ago when he was Worldwide CEO of Heinz:

66The European grocery business outside the UK will be doomed until it recognizes the importance of consumer choice – for God's sake, an average US supermarket has 30k stock keeping units, the average German supermarket 8k. To survive when you don't give the consumer what they want you need to be more than just lucky.

66 Talking of lucky reminds me of Seamus O'Ryan, the Limerick prop, who turned to me as we limped off bleeding and defeated 28 points to nil surrounded by solicitous St John's Ambulance men. 'Be Jesus Tony', he said, 'we was lucky to get nil'. 99

The ability to shift tone, pace and to show you are a real, broadminded human being and not just an automaton enables you to slip points past your audience's defences and, critically, 'play' with their mood. It may sound a little theatrical, but the best morale boosters keep you on your mental toes by denying you the certainty of what will come next – an assertion, an insight, an anecdote, a joke, or even (pray God, not to me if I'm sitting out front) a direct question to a member of the audience.

Theatrical and self-confident, they give the sense of knowing their stuff and being able to relate it to their macro-experience. Not so much morale boosters, perhaps, as lifting you to their morale level, which is deeply inquisitive, ironic and certain.

And their visual aids, which are usually sparse, attack your brain with their challenging simplicity. Tom Peters again who barks at you:

66 This is the most important formula for business today. 99

You stare bemusedly at a screen which shows you:

$$\div 2 \times 3.5 = 1.5$$

You wonder if you've gone mad – what is this?

66 Halve your workforce, more than triple per capita productivity, raise operating income by 50 per cent – it's the only way to survive today. 99

Cryptic numbers work well – like Marjorie Scardino, Chief Executive of Pearson, with her stark:

66 10 per cent 99

She was talking annual earnings per share (EPS) growth. She was talking about a promise. Morale boosting in its specificity and courage.

We move to ambience.

It's a depressing reality that most presentations take place in situations ill suited for them. Custom-built presentation rooms – ceilings too low, humid atmosphere, the clatter of coffee cups stage right and the temperature designed to induce torpor.

It's often hard to boost moral when the ambience itself is so depressing.

Two examples of ambience being used to effect.

When Volkswagen acquired the Audi distribution rights in the UK in the early 1980s, it's CEO took the dealers to a dreadful three-star hotel in the Midlands. The place was threadbare, the staff were rude, and the dealers, who were used to lavish treatment, were puzzled and irritated. The CEO mounted the rickety stage.

66 Well, have I made my point? The Audi customer expects more than you've been giving. This is how you perform now. Three-star service. I'm going to show you what you have to become. Follow me ... 99

And off they swept to a lush five-star hotel where the point was made in style.

At the first Allied Dunbar conference just after its acquisition by BAT, Sir Mark Weinberg regally presided. And what a regal morale booster he was – and still is. How can one man and his wife ooze such style and success? He would be able to persuade most people that the North Pole was a refined and trendy place to go for their summer holiday. The setting – the Wembley Conference Centre. Music by the piped band of the Black Watch. Comperes David Frost and Clive James. One long morale boost to thousands of sharply suited salespeople and independent financial advisers. Their cynicism crumbling before this extraordinary tribute to mammon. And to conclude, in reverse order of success, the top salespeople going up to receive monumental bonus cheques to the deafening strains of *Eye of the Tiger*. Boy, oh boy, did this feel rich and successful or what? Hello morale. Hello superboost.

Their cynicism crumbling before this extraordinary tribute to mammon.

Not everyone would like such an event. Way over the top and all that, but a superbly judged motivational exercise for a piratical band of life insurance salespeople. It worked. Their eyes were like cash registers afterwards.

Back to ambience and three-star hotels. Lord Tim Bell – then just plain Tim – working for Saatchi and Saatchi in its infancy as an ad agency, at the Bacofoil conference somewhere anonymous in the Home Counties. He had a slot on Roastabags (you wrapped chickens in the bag and they cooked and browned nicely). No ads to show (black mark). No budget to speak of (black mark). Nothing to say really (why bother Tim?).

Yet he spoke to salespeople (bored and fed up by now – long morning – when's the bar open?) in their own language.

66Roastabags.

Use them for wrapping old birds in (door opens, three naked women of various shapes, ages and sizes walk in and parade wrapped in Clingfilm).

Haven't done the ad yet, but how much do you think we'll spend?

OK, first week of August (for God's sake Tim, who advertises anything in August?), who'll spend most in, say, Central TV – Kelloggs, Heinz, Persil or Roastabags?99

Eventually after two 'no, no, got it wrongs' one rep timorously said 'Roastabags'.

66Well done. Right. And as a prize for you feel under your chair and you'll find a £5 note stuck there. That's it. Just go and sell loads.99

They did just that after *all* the sales reps, feeling under their chairs, realized they were £5 richer. Off they went to the breach ...

cheap trick or
an adroit piece of communication?

So was this a cheap trick or an adroit piece of communication? What Tim sussed was his audience, their mood and their need to have a simple, wickedly selective piece of information – 'On TV. Heavy spender. Bigger than the biggest brands. Stock up now.' In the 21st century trade buyers in grocery are, of course, much more sophisticated, but the principle still applies. By getting their attention, telling a simple story and boosting their wallet and their morale, Tim set off on the path to fame. Nineteen years of Tory government owed much to this simple and seductive form of thinking.

We discuss in Chapter Three how the art of giving a great presentation is no more or less than the art of telling a story. Simple plot. Engagingly told. A beginning, a middle and an end. Most presentations are in fact full of 'middle', middle and muddle. At least your morale booster has an objective – to tell a story that says, this is where we were, this is where we are and this is where we're going.

When Patrick O'Sullivan became CEO of Eagle Star he joined a company in denial. Described by one management consultant as 'Happy Valley' – and he added under his breath 'on drugs' – Eagle Star was a big, respected insurance group that was pretty well bankrupt. Patrick was the seventh, or was it eighth, CEO in as many years. So when he spoke to his team most of them expected him to be off their backs in a few months. What mystified Patrick was a permafrost layer of senior management who refused to tell those below them how bad things were, how profound the losses were. Why? Because, he learned, management were worried about denting morale by doing this. Life in Cheltenham where they were based was pretty bland – I think that's the right word – bland, overstaffed and slack. Truth was not a tool management had ever used. Patrick did – to the dismay of the obstructive and soon to be departing senior management.

Truth is funny stuff.

It can be deeply wounding and deeply frightening, but there aren't many employees who enjoy being lemmings.

By dint of energy, honesty and involvement, Patrick O'Sullivan turned the Titanic that was Eagle Star away from the iceberg it appeared to be racing so eagerly towards.

His presentations were morale boosting because they traded in realities.

His presentations were morale boosting because they traded in realities. By exposing and dramatizing the problems he created a can-do, solution-finding culture. He proved that morale boosting is not just about words (although never underestimate their importance), it's about forcing people to cheerfully face the truth. And he was – don't know how he did it – always cheerful.

How do new CEOs do that first presentation, the one which defines their shadowy existence in the company? Shadowy? Well, after all, the CEO's up there doing very important stuff and you're down here. You'll probably never see him or her again. Wrong. the CEO's up there lonely, desperate to be down here sorting it out *with* you. CEO's have been told great leaders should inspire fear, respect and love in equal measure. Chances are they get the fear bit right. You leave that first presentation terrified, hating the CEO and wondering how long either of you will last.

It should be easier than that. Here's how the presentation ought to go: This is where we were. This is where we are. This is where we're going and (critically) this is why we'll succeed in getting there. As a useful postscript this is who I am, what I've done and how I work. And the bit that makes and shapes the whole thing, the Q&A session.

The best 'where we're going – where it's all going' presenter I've ever seen is John Neil, CEO of Unipart, who seems to have exclusive use of the keyhole into the future. It's like taking a cold shower in futurology. Refreshing and exciting.

Another, quite different presenter is Leon Kreitzman, although he's a guru, not a CEO. He used to work with the

Henley Centre, the specialists in forecasting and futurism, and has written a seminal book, *The Twenty Four Hour Society*.

Leon spoke at one of those Henley Centre conferences, executives poised over notebooks noting the wisdoms of Eric Salama *et al*. He went on last. We were tired and grumpy by then. And he inspired us all with his visions of health in the future. He made us laugh, and I shall never forget the story of the South American mouse whose urine was positively, definitely fatal, and the way we were decimating the fields and forests where he had lived and he had nothing much else to do but come out and pee on you. (On reflection and after so many years it sounds profoundly unfunny. Just another example of a master presenter taking an anecdote and playing it to the mood of the audience at the time.)

Inspiring people so that they leave a presentation with lots to think about and possibly plenty to do (me? I went off and bought mousetraps) is the key to boosting morale.

Ultimately it's a substance, not a style, thing. Sure, the style can highlight the substance, but the art of rhetoric alone will quickly show up as empty of meaning.

These are not tips as such – this is not a 'how to' book – more steps to aid success.

1. Research your audience. Know how they feel, what they know, what they don't know, what they want to know.

2. Structure the story simply. And tell it like a story.

3. Get your stage and scenery right. Always use professional help, but only if you involve them in exactly what you're trying to do.

4. Find a few killer facts. Stuff no one else knows.

5. Use the audience. Talk *to* them and *with* them, not *at* them.

6. Less is more. Less is more. Cut out most of the stuff you'd love to say – it's self-indulgent most of it, you know it is.

7. Learn as you go – you can stop, pause, take stock, ask a question, change pace.

8. Make sure they know what *you* want them to *do*. No, not just feel good; leave the place and do something they otherwise wouldn't have done.

9. OK, it is showtime, whether you do it as a fireside chat or a peroration. Find ways to make it memorable for them (and you).

10. Give them something to take away that summarizes what you said. People have terrible memories nowadays.

We'll assume you're in this for more than just the money, that you have a vision of what success could be, that you enjoy what you do – especially winning.

Communicate that in
simple, enthusiastic terms.

That, in the end, is the most morale-boosting thing you can ever do.

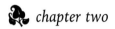 *chapter two*

A CLASSIC PRESENTATION

A guide to current malpractice

HRH KING HENRY V

St Crispin's Day 1415

Presentation to troops

Once more unto the breach, dear friends, once more;
Or close the wall up with our English dead.
In peace there's nothing so becomes a man
As modest stillness and humility;
But when the blast of war blows in our ears,
Then imitate the action of the tiger:
Stiffen the sinews, summon up the blood,
Disguise fair nature with hard-favour'd rage;
Then lend the eye a terrible aspect;
Let it pry through the portage of the head
Like the brass cannon.

Let the brow o'erwhelm it
As fearfully as doth a galled rock
O'erhang and jutty his confounded base,
Swill'd with the wild and wasteful ocean.
Now set the teeth and stretch the nostril wide;
Hold hard the breath, and bend up every spirit
To his full height. On, on, you noble English,
Whose blood is fet from fathers of war-proof –
Fathers that like so many Alexanders
Have in these parts from morn till even fought,
And sheath'd their swords for lack of argument.
Dishonour not your mothers; now attest
That those whom you call'd fathers did beget you.
Be copy now to men of grosser blood,
And teach them how to war. And you, good yeomen,
Whose limbs were made in England, show us here
The mettle of your pasture; let us swear
That you are worth your breeding – which I doubt not;
For there is none of you so mean and base
That hath not noble lustre in your eyes.
I see you stand like greyhounds in the slips,
Straining upon the start. The game's afoot:
Follow your spirit; and upon this charge
Cry 'God for Harry, England, and Saint George!'

Harry,

Will's draft has some good material but it does go on a bit (as usual) – why can't he learn to make this stuff rhyme?

Put in some graphs and generally make it a bit more lively, and it will make a good presentation.

But I'd cut it at 'brass cannon' – you'll need to keep it down to 20 minutes or so in case the French attack.

Geoffrey

Today's agenda

- Proposed strategy
- Tactical options
- Historical perspective
- Research
- Packaging
- Execution
- Summary and conclusion

Harry,

I've put this in to hold it all together; otherwise it's
going to seem a bit disorganized. A bit like
one of Will's prologues, only shorter!

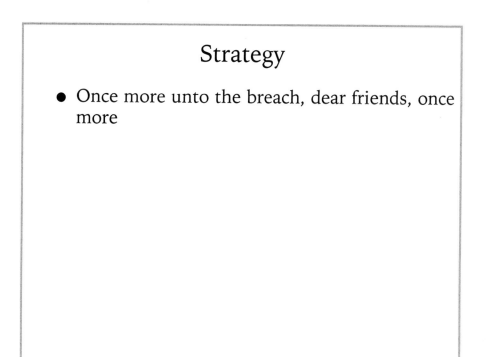

Strategy

- Once more unto the breach, dear friends, once more

H,

I've a problem with this: it's a bit patronizing. Cut out the repetition of 'once more' — always try to keep things tight. Less is more!

'Dear' is a touch familiar for this audience, and 'friends' is pushing it a bit. They know half of them will be dead by nightfall.

Perhaps a bit more detail on when, which breach, and what to do afterwards.

Can you work in a good joke like 'men, get stuck in' (i.e. stuck in the breach)?

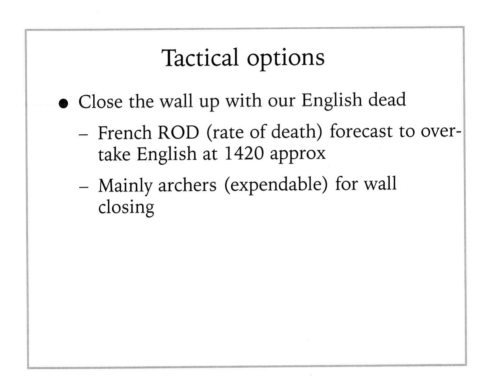

H: Very good! Makes best use of scarce resources.

Needs a few more sub-points — who is going to do this,
is it just the local dead or do we bring them in from
the camp? I like the graphs that follow.

But don't we need a few more options, just in case?
What if there aren't enough dead to fill the wall?
Would it be ethical to use French dead?

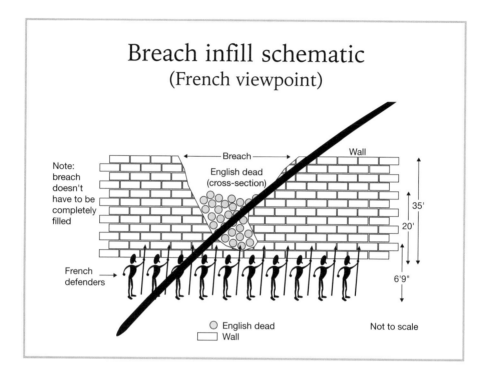

DON'T SHOW THIS!

I know a picture is worth 10,000 words and all that, but there is a time and a place.

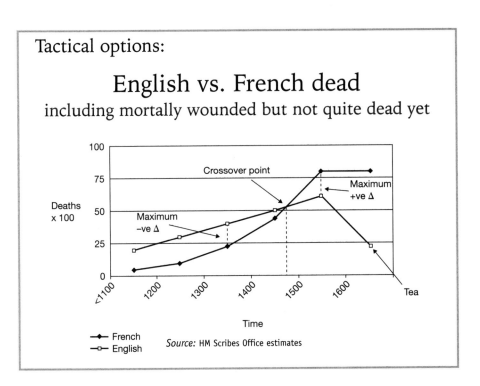

This is full of sound and fury, but what does it signify?

Tactical options:

English strategy quantification
Bull–sheep interpolated tracking model®

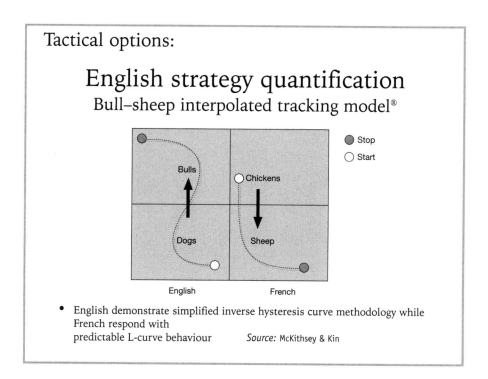

	English	French

- English demonstrate simplified inverse hysteresis curve methodology while French respond with
predictable L-curve behaviour   *Source:* McKithsey & Kin

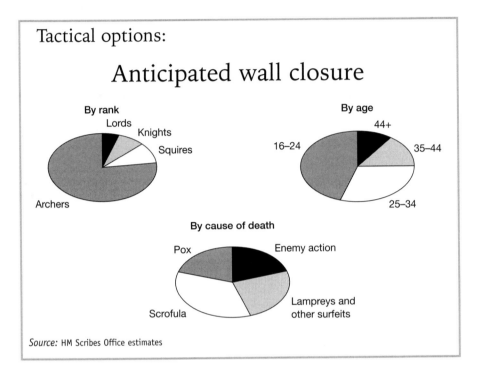

Tactical options:

Problems & opportunities

The archers

- Small due to poor food, so high mortality rate needed to achieve sufficient infill height
  Put more substantial figures in front line to bulk up wall faster (e.g. lords, squires, bards – this will also optimize press coverage)

- High hit rate among target audience
  Fill archer quivers with barbed shafts ready for early evening repeat

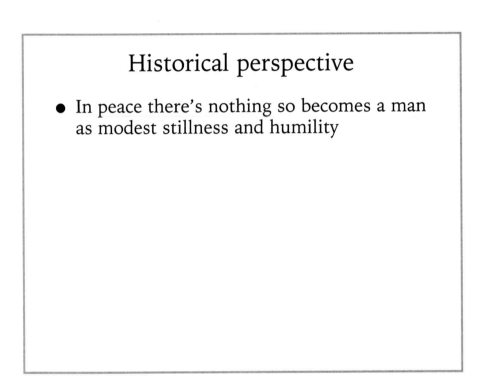

Historical perspective

- In peace there's nothing so becomes a man as modest stillness and humility

Seems a bit long-winded. Couldn't we get something in about cricket or bear-baiting? Or even sex?

Research

- But when the blast of war blows in our ears,
then imitate the action of the Tiger – stiffen
the sinews, summon up the blood

What's the Tiger got to do with this? How
many of our target audience even know the
river's in Rome?

Most of these people are going to die tomorrow.
Most of them just want to get laid. Can we
change Tiger to Goat?

Packaging

- Disguise fair nature with hard-favour'd rage

Now you're talking!
The new armour is great, by the way,
especially against slings and arrows and other
misfortunes.

Marketing plans

- Then lend the eye a terrible aspect

The eyes have it!!
Seriously, is this on strategy? Don't we want
the French to have the bad eyes? Or is this a
double bluff?
Need much more detail if we're going to get
anywhere with this. And a decent media budget.

Execution

- Let it pry through the portage of the head like the brass cannon

I'm a tinsey bit worried about this.
The brass cannon bit is good, really good. And I can see some great graphics using the cannon and the head — lots of blood and gore and stuff. The people doing the documentary tapestry will love it.
But as a call to action it is a bit tortuous, even for Will.
What about 'port-hole' instead of 'portage'? — bringing in the Navy would be good.
And 'pry' sounds a bit weak. We need something more graphic like 'smash' (now that really would make a port-hole!).

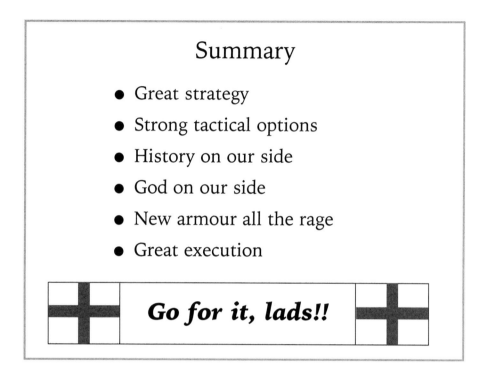

Summary

- Great strategy
- Strong tactical options
- History on our side
- God on our side
- New armour all the rage
- Great execution

Go for it, lads!!

Great stuff!
Give me excess of it!
We can't lose!

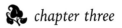

chapter three

TELLING TALES

Breaking down barriers – the importance of stories

Are you sitting comfortably? Then I'll begin.

Why are stories so important in presentations?

The answer is simple.

Presentations aren't just catalogues of information and a call for action (at least we hope not). They are about communicating with your audience, about persuading them, about bringing them round to your way of seeing a problem and thinking through a solution.

Facts are important, perhaps even critical (though, on the other hand, perhaps not); but facts penetrate the brain only very, very slowly.

Remember learning your times tables at school? Or Latin irregular verbs? Useful, of course. Essential, maybe. But slow, hard work and mind-numbingly boring. And you were much younger then.

And now you expect this audience of yours to take all these facts on board, assimilate them, come to the same conclusions as you, *and* go for the action you recommend – and all in 20 minutes. It just won't happen. The human mind doesn't work that way.

Give someone a railway timetable and they can see the point in an abstract sort of way. *Brief Encounter* it is not. Tell them the saga of your journey on the 8.19 with the broken window and the rain coming in and the man with the funny hat, and the connection you failed to get at 8.56 as there was a cow on the line called Freda so you had to get the 9.07 where you were the only man sitting in a group of 20 nuns and what they said about the ticket inspector … and even timetables can start to be the basis of life.

there was **a cow** on the line
called Freda

Stories make facts speak. They give them an emotional context. They make them digestible, even appetizing.

It is not about having a 'good' story, there is no such thing – stories are simply good or bad in the telling. But the best are always true (perhaps embroidered a little, but essentially true) and always personal. They are about your experience, your reactions, your achievements, your opinions.

'I think …' invites dialogue and engagement where 'it is …' invokes only acknowledgement.

A good comedian can pick a tiny, personal incident and build a whole act around it for ten or fifteen minutes (in fact much modern comedy seems to be founded on this idea). Presenters don't need such skills but they can learn much from watching the technique. By showing how their personal experience relates to the factual content they wish to present, they imbue it with emotional hooks for the audience to grab on to.

And there's a multiple benefit. The facts enter brains quicker, and they tend to be angled the way you want them to be, because they are viewed through your eyes. In the process you become more human, more approachable, more audience-friendly, so that the impact of all you say improves.

In the jargon, a win-win situation.

So why doesn't everyone do it? We all tell stories about ourselves all the time – listen to men in any pub or ski chalet, or women on the telephone everywhere. But most of us baulk at something so personal and revealing when we have to stand up and face a formal audience.

But when you finally bring yourself to do it, you will have broken through the barrier. You will have learned how to create common ground between an audience and yourself.

create common ground between an audience and yourself

And it is these simple little things called stories that do this. Grand oratory can't. Bluster can't. Perhaps that's why the Bible is so full of them and why it has continued to be relevant to so many people for so long. Or why *The Simpsons* continues to exert its spell over perfectly sensible grown up people.

There are of course many kinds of stories, and however brilliant, you probably aren't going to want to tell the story of the Ugly Duckling at your next salary review. But the right story creates an emotional bridge to your audience over which you can drive as big a horse and cart as you desire.

Many speakers assume that a story is just a string of anecdotes. But stories are more pervasive than that. A story has a beginning, a middle and an end; it may well be based on an anecdote, but it goes much further – it should inform your entire speech. In some respects it is akin to the running gag, but it probably isn't funny, just simply human. But like the running gag it wells up continually in one form or another. A story gives context and perspective to a presentation, and makes it particular to that speaker and that audience.

The 'beginning, middle and end' mantra defines a story in business just as it did round the camp-fires. It may start with some particular experience that captures the attention ('It was a dark and stormy night …'). Then, having grabbed the audience, it takes them on a journey, wherever the storyteller wishes. Finally, it sets them back gently on the ground, coming to a conclusion and perhaps making a particular point. It is a satisfying experience for the teller and the told. And it feels complete. A whole.

Many of the people interviewed in this book talk of the importance of telling a story. They do it in many different ways. But all of them want to move their audience from point A to point B. That is what a story does so well.

Looking around, you might think this is an age of anti story. Newspaper headlines and minimal text. The sound bite. The news review. The elevator pitch. Synthesis is all. 'Give me an executive summary' is the norm.

Yet the story still works. Because like no executive summary ever can, it provides a sense of time, a sense of cause and effect, a sense of dimension, and most of all a sense of motive.

The gossip in us all wants to know how John reacted when surprisingly told 'So after a bloodbath of a marketing campaign our market share … well John, it halved'.

Stories are about the what, the how, the why, the when and so on.

Rolf Jensen, in his forward-looking book *The Dream Society*, talks persuasively about the power of storytelling. He asserts that all business deals, all products, all brands are stories waiting to be told. And the prize goes to the person who tells the story the most convincingly.

I love Philip Larkin's definition that a story has

a beginning, a muddle and an end

That sounds like many presentations I've seen, although some simply stop rather than having an ending as such.

So how do stories fit into the world of business?

Ask Dr Spencer Johnson's bank manager. Spencer wrote *Who Moved My Cheese?* It's a story about cheese and mice and men. It's a parable about dealing with change in your work and your life, and it's the best-selling management book of all time.

Had it just been about (from the back cover) 'How to find what you want to have in life and where to look for what you want' without the mouse story, this would have been just another book about change and Spencer would merely have been very rich (he also wrote *The One Minute Manager*) as opposed to being the Croesus of management punditry.

And it's got a certain cheesy edge because the broader allegory of the story makes you think – as the magician Paul Daniels might have said, 'not a lot', but it does make you think.

It is a story with a series of messages and its capacity to conceptualize change has proved self-evidently popular.

Stories are about
tangible events
not theories.

The best speakers reach into their bag of anecdotes, of real experience, and this is what brings their presentations to life. This is what connects them to their audience, who respond with, 'That's true' or 'Could that happen to me?' or 'I just don't believe it'.

When a skilled storyteller starts telling a tale, our defences go down.

66 Are you sitting comfortably? Then I'll begin ... 99

It's a wonderfully powerful weapon.

Use it.

And let me conclude this part by telling you a story. John was a rising star at Ziptronics. Clever, charming, fast on his feet, got things done, a real high flyer.

10 March 2001 – an offsite meeting in Naples, Florida. The biggest presentation of his life. To the whole company. He was on tenterhooks.

He got to Heathrow late (terrible traffic on the M25). His passport was missing. Instead he pulled out of his pocket a crumpled note which said in childish scrawl, 'I love you daddy, please don't go away, love Luke'.

He phoned home. 'Sarah, kill Luke and then get in the car with my passport, and do it now.'

He missed the plane anyway. And the conference. And Ziptronics found pretty soon they didn't miss him when they fired him. Sarah was not amused, but then neither was Luke for a while.

John has now become a vicar because, as he says: 'I still love presentations.'

It's those sermons. Such a fantastic opportunity.

Presentations are fun.

But they're not that important.

Ask Luke

Ask John.

Ask Sarah and she'll say:

Do you know,
we all lived
happily ever after.

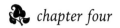

chapter four

THE PRACTICE OF PRESENTATION

Presentations are too important to busk

To many – MPs apart perhaps – the very thought of making an off-the-cuff, unprepared speech is a nightmare. It's one most of us literally have. The dream that one is on stage not having learned one's lines or of going into an exam not properly prepared.

A terror of being forced to busk.

We'd argue that you can't busk anything nowadays. And what's more buskers tend to get arrested.

The great presenters of our lifetime, the Churchills, the Macmillans, rehearsed everything. That off-the-cuff line such as

"Just a little local difficulty."

(Macmillan on his reaction to the savage knifing of half his cabinet) had like as not been carefully rehearsed several times in front of his shaving mirror.

Most of us can think on our feet (when we know our stuff).

Most of us can establish a rapport or chemistry with our audience (especially when we know them).

Some of us can even withstand a battering from the likes of Jeremy Paxman using a blend of thick skin, courage, tenacity and self-belief.

But very few of us can make a presentation to a large group of people without a significant amount of preparation and very clear answers to three questions.

- What am I trying to say – the one simple thought underlying the whole thing?
- What is the structure to my story – how many chapters, how long?
- What do I want the audience to do with what I say?
  For example:
  - Support me (vote for me).
  - Work harder.
  - Change their behaviour.
  - Learn (and use that learning).
  - Be inspired and ready to share that inspiration.
  - Buy.
  - Sell.
  - Join.
  - Leave.

The list is a long one, but decide what you want from the audience before you start preparing your presentation.

I recall a presentation I made as part of one of those elaborate advertising agency presentations to NBC Superchannel. It comprised the normal team – the planner talking about viewing habits in a new multichannel world, the account executive doing her 'trust me' piece, the creative guy showing the ads, the media guys saying why and where they'd appear.

It was a story in five or so parts – the sort of story you've heard before – a bit like a never-ending re-run of *The Archers*. I'm not even sure everyone in our team really wanted the business. Too American. Too niche. And isn't Jay Leno ghastly? (For those who don't know, he's one of America's leading chat show hosts).

My part, apart from opening proceedings and trying to tie everything together (at which I obviously failed), was to conclude proceedings with a rousing sales pitch for the business.

I must have taken leave of my senses.

I'd actually bothered to spend a whole evening watching NBC Superchannel. A curious blend of chat show, minority sport, business and soft porn.

I elaborated on this experience.

They laughed.

As I went on extemporizing and exaggerating, they laughed a lot.

I single-handedly stole whatever show we had. Rather like a brilliant but erratic midfielder dribbling from his own penalty area to the opponents' goalmouth and then (just to prove he could do it) dribbling all the way back again.

This wasn't presentation.
It was cabaret.

They dried their eyes, thanked me, left, and awarded the account to someone else.

Great orchestras, it occurred to me belatedly, do not comprise one-man-band musicians.

Presentations when done by teams need, above all else, to resemble team efforts. If not, what should look like a fine racing horse looks like a camel whose legs are of different lengths and who has been put on a tummy-troubling diet. Not, in short, a pretty sight.

Presentations done solo aren't easy. Done in teams they require four specific disciplines:

- a ruthless team leader who has the sharpest and most used blue pencil you can imagine;
- self-effacement from each team member. The task is to make the team, not the individuals look good;
- a common point of view. A common goal. If you're pitching the God account, all of you have to believe unequivocally in God (or to be perceived to believe in him);
- the ability to change pace, volume and intensity. A team presentation is a symphony.

And when you pull it off it can be quite startling in its power.

Four or five people who know their stuff, who can focus on where they're collectively going, who listen to and like each other (more important even than like is respect) and who are presenting to *you* and have their full attention on *you*. It can be hard to say no to such a group on song.

Until recently a little used word in business was 'passion'. Certainly it seemed inappropriate in laid-back Britain where a laconic understatement seemed to serve well enough. At Balliol, home to countless politicians and senior civil servants, the college mantra of 'effortless superiority' said much. However hard you try, just don't be seen to be doing so.

Leave the Americans to browbeat and rush around in a perspiring frenzy.

'Do you sincerely want to be rich?'

'Well, not really bothered actually, but I wouldn't mind a comfortable income.'

We all traded in understatement. We eschewed power talk like a hot-air balloonist avoids power lines.

Well, that's all changed.

In our new global economy where English, thank heavens, is the common language, where the possibilities of unlocking undreamed-of income streams, wealth, career options and excitement are faced daily, and where there is more money to spend than deals to spend them on, power talk is the norm.

We live in a world
of presentation.

We live in a world of presentation, of making the best of what we've got, of telling our stories to a wider and increasingly diverse audience. Ask any executive in any company how many presentations they make or attend in a year and the number will be astounding. They may give 50 or more and attend many, many more than that.

So if we work to a rough rule of thumb, which is it takes ten times as long to prepare a presentation as it takes to present it, then these executives (assuming each presentation takes 20 minutes) are spending about 10 per cent of their working year on their own presentations.

It's become a vastly important part of their lives.

Being no good at presenting is about as inexcusable as being computer illiterate or having halitosis.

Quite simply, you are unlikely to get on in life without presentation skills.

The *Financial Times* treated the whole issue very seriously a few years ago when it thundered:

Bad presentation is tantamount to fraud.

And we're not just talking about competent presentations, we're talking about brilliant ones. Those that change things – like people's minds.

Such things may well have been likely to be judged glib and over the top a few decades ago. Today we return to the Dickensian belief that a good story passionately told is money generating.

Inspirers, Perspirers, Aspirers

part one

❧

Some thoughts from master presenters based on a series of interviews

Putting a value on presentations

❧

The elevator pitch for Energis Squared

John Beaumont, Managing Director, Energis Squared

❧

Thinking out of the box

Roger Mavity, Chief Executive, boxclever

❧

The way to Carnegie Hall

Leon Kreitzman, author and guru

❧

The man who gave advertising a good name

David Abbott, former Chairman of Abbott Mead Vickers

❧

'The naked truth'

David Heslop, Chief Executive, Mazda Cars UK

❧

Why presenting shouldn't be a lottery

Dianne Thompson, Chief Executive, Camelot

Putting a value on presentations

We live in a world where people want to quantify things. The advertising executive can no longer blandly talk about enhancing key image dimensions when asked 'precisely what return on my investment can I expect?'

Sorry buster that means extra revenue, incremental operating income.

So it is with presentations.

The story of three companies and one imperative.

1. DEBENHAMS

Terry Green resigns as CEO. Share price goes down 10 per cent.

Belinda Earl replaces him and visits dozens of institutions making presentations with the Chief Financial Officer.

Share price goes up 75 per cent.

Now Belinda has a great story to tell. Ask any keen shopper and they'll say Debenhams has gone from trailing to leading retail edge.

But had anyone heard of Belinda two years ago? Would you have bought a used car from this woman? I bet you would now.

2. BARCLAYS

Martin Taylor resigns in a huff. Successor lasts one day then resigns (heart murmur). Matthew Barrett joins (and the media have a field day with his ex-wife's personal life). Things don't look good.

Add to this cash machine charges, branch closures, advertising problems and, unsurprisingly, the share price declines and prospects look dire.

Matthew speaks in person to 21,000 employees. Presents to all the institutions. Retains his sang-froid.

Today? Morale up. Share scheme uptake is high. Shares performing well.

What price a presentable, presenting chief executive?

3. UNILEVER

A piece of history. Birds Eye sales conferences used to be held at the London Palladium. Whoever was top of the bill at the time took part and Birds Eye senior management were up there with them. Bob Hope. Frank Sinatra. Tommy Cooper.

Quite simply, Birds Eye leaders were expected to play in that league.

4. THE IMPERATIVE

Research, we're told – and it sounds plausible – shows as much as 40 per cent of an average corporate image in the City can rest on the personality of the chief executive.

In such a world, presentation skills aren't an option. They're essential.

John Beaumont
The elevator pitch for Energis Squared

John Beaumont is Managing Director of Energis Squared (formerly Planet Online), one of Europe's largest Internet and eBusiness operators. The company has grown spectacularly in the past three years and is one of the leading European players in its field.

66 **Some of the things I look at when I have a presentation coming up include:**

- **the audience, who are they, what do they want from me?**
- **the message, what's the one big thing I want to say to them?**
- **what feedback do I want?**
- **how do I effectively use the time available?** 99

"Usually you know after a few moments whether the speaker is going to get his point across or not."

Until he's worked those out, John isn't in presentation mode. It takes time. For an audience, though, it works faster.

Our interviewees are divided about whether American practice is good or bad. John is a fan.

66 **Working in the US I learned the 40-second elevator pitch – how to get the key point across on the way up to the executive floor.**

People are still too often not clear in their own minds of the key point they are making. 99

However, he does criticize the tendency of US presentations to be superficial; appearing to address the point while sometimes lacking substance.

"Presentations are slicker and nowadays technology has raised the base level."

(Everyone says this – poor becomes competent, competent becomes good.)

Despite his high profile in the technological universe, John still likes acetates, writing them out by hand, keeping them short, snappy and relevant.

"Drawing graphs live in front of your audience brings them to life (and brings the audience to life too) in ways that computers cannot do."

It also displays a mastery of your material.

"Technology is beneficial if it is an *action* mechanism. Use different techniques depending on the size of the group. And whether you wish to broadcast the message, or want feedback.

PowerPoint is a bit inhuman."

(Say that again John.)

"PowerPoint is a bit inhuman."

(Could have been the title of this book.)

High-techery has done much to improve the basic level of presentations, and such things as the clarity of pictures has improved out of all recognition. But when you get down to it, presentations are not about technology.

❝All the technology in the world will never hide a poor presentation.❞

John also hates the intrusion of technology:

❝There's nothing I hate more than watching people fiddle around for five minutes setting up at the start of a show.❞

He doesn't even like build-up slides, preferring to get the chart right, ahead of time, then simply get it up on screen.

❝I focus on what I have to say. The slides are simply there to support me. I have one rule. Never read a slide to the audience.❞

His slides are sparse. Any one of them could, he feels, be expanded by a factor of four, but he resists the temptation.

❝In some presentations you feel this expansion has already been done. Everything has been spelt out to the nth degree. There's nothing left for the speaker to contribute. We are now seeing PowerPoint overload, not just more slides but the slide being used as a crutch to get through the presentation, not simply for getting the message across. This is particularly prevalent in internal middle management presentations where speakers know plenty about the topic but still feel the need for a crutch. There's also a tendency to show the amount of work done rather than the clarity of thought.❞

Civil servants, John finds, are among the worst presenters. Too often they do not really 'own' their presentations, they just seem to be reading them (and often with no great coherence or conviction).

John writes his own presentations with help from a support team to check facts and supply numbers, pictures and so on. He never relies completely on technology and always has printouts and acetates as backup.

Indeed, he would take this further – he points out that circulating notes ahead of meetings often results in better meetings. This is akin to sacrificing the drama of the presentation and the leadership position it represents, for fuller and better discussion.

(Interestingly this seems to be becoming more common and certainly demonstrates a huge sense of self-confidence on the presenter's part. 'I'll tell you the plot. Now you come to the performance.')

Obviously putting your presentation on the web is a great way of doing this, but you need good preparation if you're going to get it right.

❝The web is simply a pervasive access mechanism. And it also allows some aspects of broadcasting such as video streaming. It allows management in different locations to work together on a problem such as a presentation.❞

So despite his position as one of the leading figures in the web arena in Europe, John is cautious about its impact for the time being.

❝But in five years' time it may lead to many more interactive presentations and its multilingual capability will become more important.❞

flashy PowerPoint effects
are often inappropriate

As for web-based presentations, he finds that flashy PowerPoint effects are often inappropriate and make downloads much too slow. So the presentation ends up looking worse, not better.

Another case of not thinking about your audience.

John learned to present mainly by doing it; in particular his stay in the US taught him the value of preparing thoroughly.

66 Yes, I have had training, and I still go on refresher courses.

And I still get torn apart.

People like us can get too blasé. 99

John is an active member of the presentation culture. Presentations are critical to his life and he is highly rated as a presenter.

But reading this you know he hasn't stopped learning how to present.

And that is his biggest lesson to all of us.

Roger Mavity
Thinking out of the box

Roger Mavity is Group Chief Executive of the recently formed boxclever, the UK's largest TV rental company jointly owned by Nomura and the Granada group. He spent most of his early life in advertising refining his skills as a poacher before becoming a formidable gamekeeper. Roger thinks rather harder about business philosophy than most and confesses to having learned huge amounts from Gerry Robinson and Charles Allen, past and current chairmen, respectively, of the Granada group.

On presentations Roger is eloquent.

❝You should judge a presentation the same way you judge an advertisement.

Does it have a strong central idea?
Does it engage the audience?❞

He is a proponent of the high-risk, get-out-of-the-box school of presenters, arguing that low risk is high risk. Again, referring to advertising:

❝The only risk a low-risk ad runs is the risk no one will take any notice of it ... which, when you come to think of it, is a completely unacceptable risk.❞

That word crops up again – 'passion'.

❝You're on stage. Be theatrical. Use passionate arguments.❞

He identifies four kinds of presentation.

1. To your employees. (He finds himself doing constant roadshows – 'God knows why they'd want to listen to me' – but this is the self-effacing man who having lashed the ball 250 yards down the fairway is prone to reflect 'that's an unexpected surprise'.)

2. To your employers. (A challenging audience, this, at Granada.)

3. To your investors.

4. To make a sale.

And he believes increasingly in business that 'making a sale' is a major part of what he does. Yes, he agrees, presentations are increasingly important. Way upwards of 10 per cent of his working life.

His advice is very focused.

1. Always have a killer chart. The one that, if your audience does nothing else, you want them to remember.

A real moment of theatre:
This is the climax ... it's official.

2. Most presentations are prepared as if you score more marks for more words. Make them visual. Pictures, not words.

Make them visual. Pictures, not words.

3. Roger uses an A2 layout pad and drafts out a storyboard on one page – no detail, just the key stepping stones in the argument.

4. Write English, not 'business'.

E.g.   NOT a statement of our objectives
BUT what we're trying to do.
NOT methodological and implementational alternatives
BUT how we're trying to do it.

5. Never read the words on the chart. (People can read faster than you can speak.) Play with charts – leave things off so you can extemporize.

Never read the words on the chart.

6. If you're bringing a solution to an audience, make the problem as gloomy as possible so they say:

66 I knew sales were quite bad but I'd never realized they were as bad as this. 99

It means, as you remorselessly lead them out of the tunnel of despondency you've created, they respond to the 'only possible solution' you propose with enhanced gratitude.

7. Never define a presentation by the number of charts. Roger recalls someone saying:

66 Well this feels like a 40 chart presentation. 99

8. Draft. Draft. Draft.

66 Reduce your presentation like a good sauce. Prepare carefully two weeks ahead. Reduce the number of charts and words on a daily basis. 99

9. Most people use too much information. How often have you seen a presentation where the first half-hour elaborates on a ten-minute brief you gave?

66 In other words, don't waste time telling them what they already know. 99

10. Rehearse until you know it by heart. Know where every slide comes. Be word/slide perfect.

Roger recalls the great press Michael Portillo got at one Conservative Party Conference for speaking without notes.

66 No one commented on what he actually said but that sure as hell impressed them ... his ability to speak note- or autocue-free. 99

11. Never give out hard copies first except to market analysts who get grumpy if you don't. And with them (lawyers permitting) make sure you leave space for an uncharted passionate sell at the end.

12. Technology changes nothing.

66 Sure, you have more choice nowadays as to how to dramatize your presentation, but the underlying issues are constant and always have been. 99

Roger speaks with the authority and perception of a practised presenter (which he is). He also confesses that the process of being asked to think about presenting has made him question some of his preconceptions.

66 It is horrifying when you realize just how much of your career is dependent on presenting really well. 99

Leon Kreitzman
The way to Carnegie Hall

Leon Kreitzman is a guru. A former director of the Henley Centre, he is author of *The Twenty Four Hour Society* which was recently published and for which Leon was roundly castigated by Jeremy Paxman – inevitable that – and a rather sleepy William Deedes on Radio 4's *Start the Week*.

66 **People need sleep. Your vision of society is quite ghastly.** 99

He is also one of the world's best presenters, on call to big corporations worldwide ('I'm cheaper than Faith Popcorn, Richard, and they say I'm funnier').

On the subject of presentations he recalls the often-quoted story of the little old lady asking a New York cop: *'How do I get to Carnegie Hall?'* and he replies: *'Practice, lady, practice'*.

the more presentations you do, the better you get

Quite simply, the more presentations you do, the better you get, but Leon stresses it's about more than a presentational facility. It's about public speaking. If you're asked to speak, do it. Speak wherever, whenever you can. You'll improve simply by doing it.

Learn to be flexible.

Leon was asked to do a talk. He was briefed by the PR guy.

66 **The Chairman knows about you. He loves the philosophical approach.** 99

This made Leon feel pretty good.

The PR guy continued slightly nervously:

66 **The trouble is the Marketing Director likes a bullet point approach.** 99

'OK', said Leon, 'I'll do some philosophical bullet points.'
Leon espouses the conceptual approach.

66 **Get the idea of the thing in your head ... not the detail, not the sound bites ... the feel, the tone, the shape, the tempo.** 99

He is not alone in believing you should dream the presentation.

you should dream the presentation

He is also convinced that at the presentation event almost inevitably the weakest element will be the chairing and the introductions. The whole event will work so much better if this is perfected.

66 **Chairmen are warm-up men. They can and should create expectations in the audience. It's so much easier following a half decent introduction.** 99

He is sceptical about visual aids and the dumbing down effect of endless PowerPoint.

66 **If it doesn't stand on its own, it probably isn't worth doing.** 99

And he's apoplectic about overstaging. He talks about a major presentation he did in America.

66NCR were really generous to me. Vale, Colorado is a wonderful place to go to. The staging was worthy of George Lucas, but when they insisted on making me up I thought they'd gone too far.99

Leon Kreitzman in lipstick – a glorious thought.

He is a martinet on timing ('not a minute more, not a minute less') on the grounds that it's selfish, unprofessional and undisciplined to run over length. He cites A.J.P. 'one take' Taylor, whose early TV broadcasts always ran exactly to time.

He praises academics – much practised at lecturing. 'If they're any good, they're very, very good.'

(Interestingly David Heslop, CEO of car maker Mazda, is convinced that some of the best presenters around nowadays are headteachers. Having met William Atkinson of the Phoenix School in London's White City, who serves as a trustee on a charity I chair, Shaftesbury Homes & Arethusa, I'm sure he and Leon are both right.)

Leon reflects on humour.

66It's a king and a knave.

You know, got right, it'll be the most memorable thing you say – hook 'em in, make them remember, but get it wrong and you're toast.99

We recall Lady Trumpington, former leader of the House of Lords, who said:

66The great thing about someone with a sense of humour is you're always listening to hear what they say next.99

Leon's two favourite presenters are Harold Macmillan (again) and J.K. Galbraith. The first because he understood his craft so well. Witness his lovely story about hand movements. Basically he said if you can't do it, don't move them, but if you can, remember the hand used in emphasis makes its movement *before* the words come out.

❝Curiously, Hugh Gaitskill, one time leader of the Labour Party, used his hands to emphasize after his words. Very odd effect.❞

J.K. Galbraith is measured, calm and still, and enormously authoritative. He speaks slowly, with a dry wit. At the time of writing he is 91. He is a Scots Canadian which is relevant because Leon has less time for the American school of presentation and, if you live in the USA, mark this well before presenting in Europe.

❝The Americans tend to shout in presentations. They approach the thing like a sledgehammer approaches a nut.

And they give the same presentation irrespective of context (e.g. if World War III has been declared, they give the same presentation as they would on a perfectly normal day).❞

He has the right to an opinion on American presentations, years back having been executive assistant to the vice president of Ford Europe and witness, therefore, to the juggernaut known as the 'Ford presentation'. Ford is said to be to presentations what the Spanish Inquisition was to religious tolerance.

This, mind you, was in the days when it took more than two hours to alter a slide, compared to two minutes or less nowadays.

To be fair, Leon speaks fondly of the Ford attention to detail where, when Henry Ford II was being presented to by senior executives, there were 14 slide projectors working an elaborate gavotte with each other and another 14 matching projectors all with their lens covers on – just in case.

He ends his observations noting sadly that presentation technique tends to be more important than content and more worryingly that an adept presentation achieves a validity in its own right where, somehow, $1 + 1 = 3$ as a slide can be made to look right.

presentation technique tends to
be more important than content

It is, he reflects:

66 a little like the corporate meeting where someone asks 'how long will this meeting last?' rather than 'what is this meeting designed to achieve? 99

Anyone who's seen Leon at work will attest to the power of humour, brevity and content. But then again, he speaks to us. He doesn't exactly present. He's too experienced for that.

David Abbott
The man who gave advertising a good name

David Abbott became the youngest managing director of Doyle Dane Bernbach at the age of 28, was a founder member of French Gold Abbott and then the legendary Abbott Mead Vickers of which he was chairman until he retired. David writes like a dream. He's probably the finest prose writer of the past two decades (no, I'm not joking). Remember all those glorious Sainsbury's and Volvo ads? Intelligent, witty, focused, and full of integrity.

David is also a very nice man and a brilliant presenter.

When he speaks, you listen.

He describes his world of advertising as 'full of brave presentations and horrendous mistakes' and describes pitching for the Metropolitan Police account. Three senior people arrived and David greeted them:

66 'Ello, 'ello, 'ello. 99

Laconically he observes the agency didn't get the business. David's most endearing and infuriating quality is his constant desire to embrace the absurd.

66 Make people laugh early on in the presentation.
Be mischievous.
Playfulness is an important part of life much neglected by many in business. It helps both speaker and audience empathize with each other.
Anyway, self-deprecating stories can take the edge off problems. 99

(I recall a senior civil servant telling me just how funny Harold Wilson and Jim Callaghan were in meetings as the pound ran into big trouble in the seventies. Self-deprecation helped keep them sane. More than you could say for the pound.)

David recalls the youth in a yellow body stocking wearing a gigantic wedge of look-alike cheese whose role was to dramatically enter at the climax of a pitch for the Dutch Cheese Marketing Board.

Cue the youth.

No entry possible.

Door too small.

Pitch unstitches.

66**Much to do with good presentations is about sensible planning and basic politeness.**99

Questions to ask:

- What was the original brief?
- What was on the client's mind when he prepared it?
- Have you read, re-read, re-read it – constantly gone back to this one fixed point in your relationship?
- If you are departing from it, have you decided exactly how to justify that and manage the client's expectations?
- Have you really thought about the audience:
  —their age (ages)
  —likes/dislikes
  —preferences for formality/informality
  —male/female
  —how many
  —common interests
  —what did they hear last time?

David then sets some rules which he has applied and, given his success, seem worth studying carefully.

1. Field as small a team as possible. Never field passengers.

2. Present to the whole room, not to the person you think is the key decision maker. You might be wrong and it's impolite anyway.

3. Create intimacy.

4. Check timings. Check equipment. Be prepared to abandon things if they're not working.

5. Tell the audience what you're going to do and what ground you're going to cover at the outset. (David always invited interruptions. I recall the French Gold Abbott mantra: 'We want to have a dialogue, not a monologue.')

6. A strong narrative drive is important. 'Remember,' he says, 'you're building a case, not proving you've done a lot of work.'

   Build up, lead inexorably to a conclusion and if you do this right the conclusion appears natural.

A strong narrative drive is important.

7. Avoid clichés.
   Of course you want the business. Of course you found it fascinating. Make your fascination evident in the work.

8. Sit or stand? Rule of thumb says stand if there are more than four in the room.

9. If you've got charts, read them. Word for word. But read them as soon as the chart appears and the audience will absorb your message at your pace. If you don't do this, the audience will race ahead of you and be impatient for the next chart. If you have to elaborate, do it after you have read the chart, never before.

David believes you need charts much less often than you think. He recalls the daunting Peter Prior of Bulmers, the cider makers and drinks company, who once interrupted him as he started presenting from charts:

❝I can have an ordinary conversation with you and remember what you say. So why the charts? Why are you treating me like an idiot?❞

Charts are too often used to comfort the presenter rather than illuminate the audience.

10. Watch, listen, be intuitive about your audience. Honesty really works. David quotes Bill Bernbach, probably the most famous advertising pundit of all time and founder of Doyle Dane Bernbach:

❝A small admission earns a large acceptance.❞

David reflects on chemistry. He always seems relaxed and self-deprecating. What he says is important but not too serious. He notes that many presenters get into presentation mode.

❝They adopt strange, contorted behaviour ... put on special voices and stop being human beings.❞

DAVID ABBOTT

Even when things go wrong, good chemistry can save you. He recalls having to justify using posters for K Shoes, an account his agency had won without pitching. David was a creative man. Media was not really his forte. He confesses to having waffled and dug himself deeper and deeper.

66 **Posters are a universal medium … in fact the only person who wouldn't be influenced to buy a pair of shoes from a poster would be a one-legged man.** 99

Only then did he remember that the marketing director sitting opposite was a one-legged war hero. David ruefully reflects:

66 **In the circumstances he was really very nice about it.** 99

Presenting for business – selling presentations – is very competitive.

66 **A climate of winning is important and can lead to extraordinary success. How the room looks and feels is critical. Never present in basements. (Why do people do this? It leads to 'bunker mentality'.)** 99

David wants:

66 **Daylight, flowers, clean waste paper baskets … an atmosphere that's positive before you start.** 99

As Chairman of AMV, David had to talk to the City.

I tried not to compartmentalize our audiences. We presented a consistent brand and consistent behaviour whoever we were talking to. Our annual reports reflected this.

❝As far as analysts were concerned we always tried to keep it informal and light-hearted. They knew the figures in advance and we had a good record of meeting their expectations, so this wasn't too difficult.❞

David always made presentations a pleasant experience. It wasn't just that he was sincere: he knew what was good. Unsurprisingly, he says:

❝I couldn't sell an ad I didn't like.❞

He probably couldn't sell to a client he didn't like either.

Most of all, he always seemed to be a man who gave clients the best advice he could.

Anyone who can achieve that kind of credibility is likely to make a pretty convincing presenter and give their industry a good name as well.

At moments like this (too much praise for the man, too much pomposity), David would have sought and found a deflating observation or even a biting aside. It is a sound presentation point. You need sour as well as sweet to communicate properly.

David Heslop
'The naked truth'

The most difficult thing for most of us is finding our 'own voice' when we present. How often have we heard a Dalek on the podium? Is this automaton married with three lovely children? Is he/she a passionate human being with views of his/her own? Yet (if he/she is) why does he/she sound like a BT computer message? Is it nerves or is it simply an act of omission – an omission in deciding how to act 'being yourself'?

Comedian Jack Dee described on Radio 4 how he found his performing voice through a series of failures. He found he could write the stuff but when it came to delivering it well on stage, as he put it:

66 **Yes, they laughed at all the jokes but at absolutely nothing in between. Quite simply audiences didn't find *me* funny.** 99

So he decided to give up life as a stage performer and focus on writing material for other people. He had three or four gigs to fulfil his contract so he did them but with lacklustre attitude.

For Jack, lacklustre rang cash registers and created waves of laughter. The 'don't give a shit' delivery became the 'voice' that rocketed him to stardom.

So how do *you* do it?

David Heslop, CEO of Mazda Cars UK, carries his process of self-discovery to extremes. David is a large, impressive man who thinks deeply about how things work. He is unmistakably a new world thinker who is always reaching out for the new, new thing. But remember, I said he was large. Larger than life and physically large. He says:

66 **Whenever I have to do a presentation I practise in the nude in front of a full length mirror. There's nothing more daunting, no audience more frightening, than yourself in the buff.** 99

As regards the 'voice' we all seek, he simplifies the vision.

❝Always speak to one person. If there are a thousand in the audience, think of one person you're talking to.

You can't *talk* to a crowd.❞

Interestingly, many advertising copywriters say the same. Fix on the idea of one person, a confidante such as your spouse, child, mother, father, and address your thoughts, wishes and ideas to that person.

David espouses the cause of passion and belief:

You have to believe what you're saying even when you don't believe it.

His best ever presentation?

❝Sounds daft, but it was a speech I made to the woman and the team around her who helped deliver my first child. It came from the centre of my being, not from the side of my mind.❞

David gives three tips on presenting, focusing on people and how they feel:

1. *Empathize*. How do they feel? Why are they here? What's on their mind?

2. *Personalize*. Make it real and specific for them. Talk *with* them not to them.

3. *Never patronize*. So easy to do. Boss addresses employee (patronizes probably). Expert presents to non-expert (patronizes often).

And he makes one general observation about preparation and preparedness.

❝You have to know *why* you're doing it and *what* (in simple terms) you're trying to get across.

Simplistically, know both the point and the points.❞

And has it changed? Technology means today's presentation in the theatre is tomorrow's piece on the Internet and the advances of the more obvious kinds – autocues, animation, video, etc. – mean it's easier to hold interest and look good but the essential truths about how to carry off a presentation are unchanged.

In the final analysis a presentation is about *giving*. If you give, and do so in a way that sparkles, your audience will take away more than a few thoughts. They may actually change the way they do things and the way they think.

David, in common with many CEOs, spends much of his life presenting, to his dealers, to his staff, to industry bodies.

Like all of us he has good days and not so good days. One of his best (not natal this time) was, he says, to the *Independent* on the theme 'Black + White = Purple'.

I eyed David with well-practised suspicion. Was he too many glasses into a fine claret?

'Purple, David,' I said 'very good.'

Then he explained. And it isn't good, it's brilliant.

David was asked to speak to the classified and display advertising sales people on the *Independent* newspaper. He decided to broadly base his theme on the fact that they were rather dull (well it sounds a dullish job, doesn't it?) and being in the newspaper business were making black and white equal (as it usually does) grey.

He wanted them to think bigger, better, more colourfully and make black and white equal purple. Since then 'purple' has been an internal codeword at the *Independent* for thinking out of the box.

But the best part of the story wasn't this at all. It was about true connection with an audience.

Late in the day he'd discovered the audience he was going to address was rather larger than he'd been led to expect (350, not 20) and, viewing his carefully crafted slides, he realized they spoke to the need to do a presentation, not to the audience in question. When it came down to it he simply didn't know this audience at all.

they spoke to the need to do a presentation, not to the audience in question

He gloomily surveyed the likely outcome. Big man from Mazda strides in, makes rousing but irrelevant oration, misleadingly loud applause as he strides out is followed by a collective 'What was that all about?' reaction.

David is nothing if not brave. As he surveyed himself in the nude in front of his full-length mirror, he decided the presentation had to go.

He called the guy at the *Independent* who'd asked him to speak and said: 'Do me a favour. Put me up in the hotel the night before, don't tell anyone who I am and get me a piano ...'

'Do you want some boy scouts and a ball of string too?'

'Don't be silly. Just a piano.'

David is an accomplished musician. So from 7.30pm until 2am he simply played the piano in the bar. The guys from the *Independent*, with increasingly drunken candour, told their all to this versatile and charming pianist. They had singsongs, they laughed, they cried, they stood around the piano and applauded Dave. Dave the pianist.

By 2am there wasn't much David didn't know about his audience collectively and individually. What was on their minds and in their hearts.

So when he walked on stage next morning, there was a momentary reaction of: 'Oh my God, it's that piano player. It can't be. I'm hallucinating. Am I still drunk?'

Oh my God, it's that piano player.

But David was on a connectivity winner. 'Good morning everyone. I got fired as the pianist so I've taken over as CEO of a car company. Real come down but never mind ...

'Now I want Susan, Fred and Harry to come up on the left of the stage and Phil, Debbie and Claire to come up on the right of the stage ...'

The monotone of most presentations was transformed.

Black and white became purple.

David takes the subject of presenting seriously (but with David seriously is always accompanied by an exuberance of spirit, not a frown). He shares his passions and beliefs with a naked intensity. At least we can understand in part how he manages to generate this.

'Try it,' he urges. 'Get your kit off and speak in front of that mirror – it's eerie.'

I did. He's right. And not a pretty sight.

Dianne Thompson
Why presenting shouldn't be a lottery

Dianne Thompson, CEO of lottery organizer Camelot, is one of my heroines. I adore her for her tenacity, courage and cleverness and for preventing her success from tarnishing her femininity and niceness. You could say I am a bit of a fan.

She says something quite obviously true but also chilling for would-be presenters.

There is no excuse for any presentation being boring nowadays.

She used to be scared of presenting, she says; now she is just appropriately nervous.

66It's good to let a bit of adrenalin kick in.99

She likens presenting to learning to drive.

66Do you remember what it was like changing gear? There always seemed to be too much to do. Eventually it becomes second nature.99

And she reiterates the point that

the more you present.
the better you get

DIANNE THOMPSON

Dianne, unlike many in her position, always writes her own script and rehearses assiduously, although not as assiduously as Don Sloan, her one-time boss at Woolworths, who honed his presentations for hours and hours, taking out words, moving from twenty words to five.

❝Don't you think that's going a bit over the top – likely to take out the naturalness as well as the words?❞

The worst presentations are those that ramble and fail to keep to time. (Dianne is emphatic that sticking to a timetable is critical, in fact the evening of this interview she was appearing in front of a planning committee – not Camelot business – with exactly three minutes to speak. Green light means start. Red light means stop. Undisciplined timing meets its nadir in such situations.)

The best presentations always contain passion and enthusiasm, such as that given by Barbara Cassani, CEO of low-cost airline Go. Dianne had heard her recently and said she was:

❝Witty, concise and interesting.❞

The perfect recipe for a good presentation.

Of all audiences she had always thought the media the most difficult. In her early days at Camelot she was mauled by the media – she describes the hostility of one press conference as almost tangible. Today she says 'they're really nice'. (I think she underestimates the power of her presentations over time and the fact that she comes across as a person of total integrity. It's hard to be nasty to someone so nice.)

She invests a lot of money in training at Camelot and has a specific Professional Presentations course.

She describes how a colleague was transformed from a rambler with poor body language into a star presenter. How?

❝It was down to training, to learning to prepare better and to letting the latent enthusiasm and passion communicate itself.❞

Technology has changed dramatically and for anything major you must, she insists, employ experts. But with the advent of PowerPoint and other software, the stakes have risen.

Dianne likes visual aids.

❝They can brighten things up and give the audience a different point of focus than simply having to stare at you.❞

She used to use autocue but abandoned it because she found it too artificial.

❝It gets in the way. Nothing in a presentation should ever do that.❞

Her speeches are always typed

- broad margin on left (for notes, slide changes, etc.)
- double-spaced
- 18 point.

And renouncing vanity she always wears spectacles.

When asked who she'd like to be as a presenter if she could wave a magic wand, she is silent for several seconds.

❝I quite like being me – does that sound vain (no it doesn't, you're the least vain person I know – Ed.) – but I wish I could be more witty and could handle humour better.❞

She really shouldn't worry. The firestorm she's been through has turned her into one of Britain's best-known and best-liked CEOs. (Recently she was voted Businesswoman of the Year).

She has found her own voice. And that's what all great presenters do.

❧

part two

PRESENTATIONS THAT INSPIRE

OR CONFUSE OR SIMPLY SELL

🐾 *chapter five*
'I'm your boss – now what was it you wanted to tell me'   *79*

🐾 *chapter six*
'I'm your boss – trust me, follow me, respect me'   *82*

🐾 *chapter seven*
The shining white teeth of the super salesman   *91*

🐾 *chapter eight*
The final analysis   *105*

🐾 **INSPIRERS, PERSPIRERS, ASPIRERS**   *115*
Interviews with master presenters

Mike Kirsch	– *Norwich Union Life*
Chris Pinnington	– *Euro RSCG Wnek Gosper*
Lucas van Praag	– *Goldman Sachs*
Simon Skeldon	– *Taylor Nelson Sofres*
Dr Neville Bain	– *Consignia*
Michael Ullmann	– *INSEAD*
Marcus Alexander	– *London Business School*

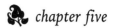 *chapter five*

'I'M YOUR BOSS – NOW WHAT WAS IT YOU WANTED TO TELL ME?'

Finding a common language

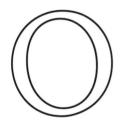ne of the most daunting experiences most of us face is to present to the board or, in a way worse, one to one to our boss, or our boss's boss or our boss's boss's boss.

It's career on the block time and it's not our hand on the cleaver.

It's career on the block time
      and it's not our hand
            on the cleaver.

Your point of view	Their point of view
Responsibility	Power
Defendant	Prosecutor
Knowledgeable	Ignorant (on this subject)
Clever	Smart
Frightened	Bored
Enthusiastic	Distracted
Lots to say	Hard of hearing: bad at listening
Conditioned to say 'yes'	Conditioned to say 'no'
This is important	What am I doing next?
Why's he so grumpy?	Why's he so cocky?

So it isn't going to be an easy confrontation.

What's patronizing to one is avuncular to the other. What's passionate to one is gauche to the other. What's exciting to one is distracting to the other.

It would help if both parties bothered to find out or could find a mechanism to understand their respective agendas. Because when they do the presentational relationship will be a lot more productive.

So, some simple advice to each party:

You	Them
Keep it simple	Give them full attention
Keep it structured	Don't interrupt too much
Cover the upsides and downsides	Quiz numbers
Cover key issues	Ask if that's all
If you are trying to achieve something, say precisely what	Be receptive
And say it twice	Make a joke
Watch body language	Be relaxed
Listen	Listen
Remember 'win wars, not battles'	Say 'yes', 'no' or 'maybe subject to …'
End by summarizing what's happened, going to happen, and next action	Encourage
	SAY THANK YOU

The two most important phrases in the management lexicon are:

Well done

and

Thank you.

So thank you for reading this.

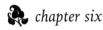

chapter six

'I'M YOUR BOSS – TRUST ME, FOLLOW ME, RESPECT ME'

Delivering the message

ou know the story about messages being passed along the trenches in World War I – what starts off as 'Send reinforcements, we're going to advance' becomes after a few iterations, 'Send three-and-fourpence, we're going to a dance'.

This still happens today. Only it's usually to presentations originated by the chief executive.

Typically, this pre-eminent piece of corporate communication gets sent to senior managers for them to give to their staff. Very sensibly they fine-tune it to remove the bits that aren't relevant to their team and enhance the bits that are.

They in turn then pass it on, so that it cascades down level after level, with the original message getting more and more diffuse (or, depending on your point of view, more and more relevant) as it goes.

By the time it reaches the foot-soldiers – the people who face the customers or suppliers on a day-to-day basis, the salesmen and women, the receptionists, the telephone operators who probably do most to make the new corporate message real to the outside world – what is left?

A summary of a summary of a summary. Nothing.

Worse, by this time it is no longer the chief executive talking to me, the doorman. It is often corporate-speak at its worst. What should inform and motivate, what should be something to take home and show the family so you can say 'look at the great guys I work with' and they'll be interested and even agree, is simply ... well, boring.

It may have been quite boring at the outset – sadly, corporate presentations too often are. Put together by committee, politically too correct, full of safe corporate-speak and frequently less than inspired. But sure as hell it can be really boring by the end of the process.

Boring used to mean worthy. Now it means dead. And a waste of a huge amount of time, money and effort.

What effect does the presentation have? Done well it shows management in touch with, learning from, and caring about their workforce. It manifests itself in loyalty and commitment. Done badly it reinforces the view that senior management are out of touch with those at the coalface. Them and us.

Roxy Fry of Trinity Management Communications has given a lot of thought to the drivers of internal communications. She emphasizes the importance of apparently small things: the real signature on the letter, the status of the group assembled (and where they are assembled), the breadth or otherwise of the recipient group ('oh, this went to everybody so it can't be very important', or 'this only went to a few senior people, and to me, so they must think I'm important too').

So with a little care you can make the *person* important, not just the message.

Let's look at three examples.

Going down the line

Not many CEOs of large companies can possibly get to all their employees on a regular basis, but some certainly try.

At Pearson, for example, top management tour major locations as soon as the annual results are announced. 'Of course, we don't see everyone,' says Marjorie Scardino, Chief Executive, 'but we have a damn good go. It's exhausting – sometimes we have given about a dozen presentations in three or four days – but it goes with the territory.' The territory in this case may include at least five countries and three languages.

She makes the point that staff are encouraged to ask questions; for those who feel too intimidated to speak out in front of large groups of their peers, e-mails are available and always receive a personal reply.

'If we are really going to be what we claim – the best company in the world to work for – we can only make it real if communication is genuinely a two-way process. Is it worth it? Yes, of course it is. It is one of the single most important jobs we do as managers.'

Why doesn't she delegate this? Two reasons.

'All these meetings are done by me or a senior board member. It is important that we don't become remote from the people who do the real work in the company. We need to see and be seen. I'm interested in everything about this company and everyone who works for it.

It is one of the single most important jobs we do as managers.

'And I learn much more from them than they do from me. They're the ones who get the business, create the content, design the space, do the deals on a day-by-day basis. I can't do any of that. It's they who are out there talking to customers every day.'

In this case the end-of-year results presentation developed for analysts is reworked to make it more interesting and relevant to staff, dropping technical charts and adding interesting videos, TV interviews, new advertising commercials from different countries, discussions of new web sites and so on.

So although the presentation is based on existing material, it is targeted firmly at its new audience. It is issued to each presenter (translated if necessary), but few if any changes are made from country to country.

There is no set text for each speaker to follow. Each audience has its own needs and each speaker finds his or her own voice. But the visuals themselves ensure consistency of message, that the necessary ground is covered and that nothing important is omitted.

Star of page and screen

What if you can't get to meet the staff? Olivier Fleurot is Managing Director of the *Financial Times* newspaper, with 40 offices around the world and a business based around daily printing, distribution and delivery deadlines that would make most men blanch.

The newspaper industry is fast-moving and unforgiving. And the FT has been growing faster than most, launching new editions in market after market. It has built up a worldwide operation and the MD needs to give a regular review of the business to his staff across the globe. But he simply cannot get round them all quickly enough for the message to be consistent as well as up-to-date and relevant.

'Employees are becoming more demanding,' Olivier says. 'They are more mature and they know more about the business. I talk to people all the time. You can never communicate enough.'

'But the review is different. I like to get it to everyone at the same time, both to make sure it is today's news as that's our culture, and so that no one feels left out in the cold.'

He used to make a presentation to his head office staff, video it, and distribute the video. But the result wasn't what he wanted. 'It is of course the simplest solution,' he says. 'But the problem is that even the most riveting live presentation makes for very bad video viewing. Think of it – 20 minutes of me droning away on tape would put even my mum to sleep!'

Few executives are comfortable in front of the camera and even the most charismatic and effective live speaker can look stilted and lifeless on the TV screen.

The solution was fairly straightforward – use the live presentation as the basis for the video (after all, it contained all the key messages, statistics and other information, and all the arguments had been carefully clarified and refined). Olivier needed to be seen to be at the centre of things so he was filmed discussing each of the key presentation points in turn. A formal script was unnecessary.

Unremitting head-and-shoulder shots quickly become boring and there are few who can get away with what playwright Alan Bennett does so effortlessly. So existing video footage from the corporate video, commercials (including out-takes) and so on were trawled for segments that would illustrate the new video and add impact.

A camera crew, booked for a day, filmed Olivier, then spent the rest of the day filming people. Putting faces to any people mentioned by name. Showing people doing ordinary day-to-day things in the different departments mentioned. Showing people coming in through reception, into the canteen at lunchtime; people asking or answering questions; people milling about and doing unusual or amusing or unexpected things.

Always people.

An editor quickly cut the material together. And within a day or two the videos were approved and on their way.

Video material from other offices can be incorporated to build on everybody's fascination with how the other half lives, seeing how their opposite numbers do their jobs, putting faces to people only spoken to on the phone. In short, building a community of common interest.

So for the staff worldwide,

the corporate video becomes a video about 'us', no longer a video about 'them'

The brewer's tale

In the early nineties, it became clear to Whitbread management that the more they examined the future of their business, the less promising it looked.

Whitbread, one of Europe's great brewers, had been brewing since 1742. It owned and operated pubs all over Britain, with national and local brands and fierce local loyalties. It had invested in plant and distribution systems and management and staff on a huge scale.

But the beer business was beginning to change radically. The demographics were starting to waver – fewer in the right age group, fewer in the right social group, a trend to foreign bottled beers, to new brands, to a remorselessly increasing breadth of brands. Worst of all a growing interest in health and fitness. In a broader definition of leisure, 'a night out with the boys' was turning into 'a meal out with the family'.

How should or could a traditional production-led brewer react?

And once the key group of decision makers had agreed on how to react, how did they go about changing the entire culture of the organization, a culture deeply embedded and strongly held? If they didn't succeed, there was every chance that the company would simply wither away.

changing the entire culture of the organization

At that time Whitbread made half its profits from drink manufacturing. It is now no longer in that business. It's in hotels, active leisure and restaurants – none of which, apart from a small restaurant business, existed then.

In 1992 David Reed, a former Labour MP, was hired as Communications Director to manage this process of change at Whitbread; not just among staff, but right through the chain, including investors. If the owners of the company didn't buy into the solution, there was no solution.

> Our task was to make sure that our stakeholders knew what we were trying to do and, preferably, supported it.

Many people were involved in this process. Peter Jarvis was Whitbread's Managing Director at the time and gets most of the credit for this effective transformation, but he is the first to insist that it was a team effort and the result of years of work by a great many dedicated people.

> Chief among the problems were the over-protection of management and the belief that the owners were financial institutions just after the best returns.

The first thing they had to do was to ensure that senior people throughout the company really understood the problem.

> We elevated the process of communication from being a minor by-product of the business to a major function.
>
> We had to learn – and respond to – what the market wanted to know.
>
> And we had to make sure people understood that the share price was not a reward for past performance.

They discovered they were often doing the very things shareholders wanted but were simply not communicating it to them. So they instituted an annual strategy presentation where they looked at the markets they were in, where they were moving, and how their brands were performing.

Since 1993 they have gone on the road at least once every year having face-to-face meetings with existing and prospective shareholders.

❝Face-to-face presentations were the most important tool. When you look someone in the eye, they can quickly make up their minds if you're spinning them a line or really mean it. Ninety thousand copies of *The Whitbread News* were issued each month. It was well read by management and people in offices, and people in the pubs like getting it. 'Somebody is at last trying to communicate with us.' 'Do you read it?' 'No, but we like getting it.❞

Whitbread was one of the first UK companies to make use of the Internet to convey information around the company quickly and accurately. This had a big effect on team briefings. It led management to redefine corporate responsibility so that managers had proper information to brief their people. Now every year they interview 25,000 staff to look at job satisfaction and so on, so they know the briefing process is working.

In the end presentations have become a critical tool for Whitbread, which it uses well. At a more fundamental level, however, David is quite clear:

"The real contribution presentations make is in forcing you to clarify in your own mind what it is you are trying to say."

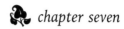

chapter seven

THE SHINING WHITE TEETH OF

THE SUPERSALESMAN

The sales pitch

Most of us hate the hard sell. We may laugh at Arthur Daley but we don't want to meet him in real life and we certainly don't want to be described as being like him. The hard sell is characterized by the salesman being a winner and the buyer a loser.

We used to buy things from shops that had salesmen, people who demonstrated products. We had more time. Now we live in what JKR, the UK design agency, calls 'the one-second society' where we shop on the run. Now we rush round supermarkets serving ourselves with, maybe, half-remembered advertisements urging our hands in one direction rather than the other. Or we surf the net. Salesmen with their toothy grins and Mr Sincerity suits don't interrupt our buying musings. We the consumer, the buyer, are in charge. At last.

Yet successful and unsuccessful sales presentations happen every day. How did that company get its product on the supermarket shelf? Not by thought transference but, like as not, by a thoughtful sales presentation. How did that web site raise the money to seduce you with its graphics and, well I never, sales messages? By persuading a venture capital fund or a corporation to fund its work. By presenting them with a good idea. By selling them.

salesmanship is more important than ever before

In a world moving as fast as ours, where the 'new, new thing' is out of date before you've registered its existence, salesmanship is more important than ever before. Try reading *The New New Thing* by Michael Lewis, the author of *Liars Poker*. It tells the story of a man, Jim Clark, who made $1 billion out of three start-up companies in relatively quick succession. That's right – $1 billion out of each. Most of us would be delirious with success like that; Jim merely seems a bit surly. His last company, Healtheon, which set out to revolutionize the US health business through dedicated computer technology, was the product of a one-chart or envelope presentation which, as I recall, went as follows.

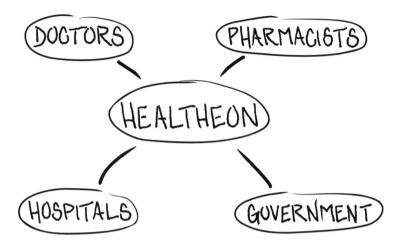

Now that looks to me like a takeover bid. And if I, on my proverbial envelope, went to John Prescott and said, 'Right, Secretary of State, I have here the answer to all your problems.'

(He was in charge of transport when we wrote this.)

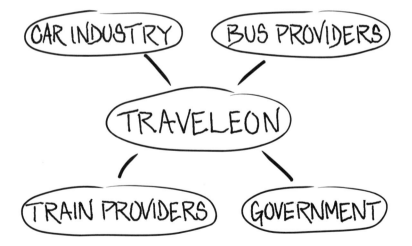

I rather fancy John's response would have been a swift left hook. Yet were we Jim Clark ('he's made $2 billion already … he has the Midas touch for himself and all around him'), maybe not.

Jim's lesson to us all? Track record and simplicity.

Remember Margaret Thatcher's immortal line about Lord – then merely David – Young, her former Trade and Industry Secretary.

David brings me **solutions.** Other people bring me **problems.**

So the key principle of any great sales presentation is that it has to bring a solution, even if it's to a problem that hasn't yet been recognized as such or in that way.

Let's distinguish between the different kind of sales presentations.

- The beauty parade. A competitive credentials pitch.
- An analytical or creative contest. Between design, PR or advertising companies.
- A 'do this now please' sales pitch. Usually small audience – generally specific, simple sell.
- A 'cold canvass' big sell. A big idea – Healtheon – presented to a series of inscrutable, sceptical, do-we-need-innovation audiences who are there reluctantly.
- A perfectly normal reporting presentation with an edge. 'Oh and there's one other thing … can you increase the overdraft?'
- A presentation in a series which reports activity and which has the hidden agenda of leading to a big sell some time in the future.

- A fishing trip. A presentation designed to elicit a response from the audience which clarifies what exactly they will and won't buy.

Much has been written of the psychology of buying and selling. In Michael Crichton's *Rising Sun* he explores, in the context of this thriller, the ambivalent attitude of the Americans to the land-grab buying strategy of the Japanese in California in the Eighties and counterpoints it with the view of Akio Morita, founder of Sony:

66 If you don't want us to buy it, don't sell it. 99

In the sophisticated 21st century, of course, virtually everything is for sale – at a price. It is possible to construct almost any kind of deal, alliance, transfer of assets to gain strategic focus. Yes, anything is possible. Which means in some form or another every presentation is a current, latent or prospective sales pitch. Which also means virtually all senior executives are spending as much time trying to divine hidden meanings and strategies in each other's presentations as they do in managing their businesses.

virtually everything is
for sale – **at a price**

Even the blunt, old-fashioned

66I mean what I say and I say what I mean99

is likely to evoke a mystified:

66What exactly did he mean by that?99

Back to the different kinds of sales pitches.

1. The beauty parade

This is where three things count.

- *Who knows who* and who knows what about whom because reputation makes a difference.
- *First impressions*. These are called 'beauty parades' for a good reason. How you look, how you dress, your body language, all count. We all know it's the first minute of an interview where the seeds of doubt or approbation are devastatingly sown. But also bear in mind what it is you're selling. Richard Eyre, former ITV boss, tells the story of appointing a company to do the web site for Capital Radio (which he then ran).

66They were unprepossessing. The team leader seemed to be 13. His colleague had a shaven head, rings in his ears and nose, said nothing, simply glared at us. The team leader told us: 'You don't want to be at the leading edge or even at the cutting edge. You want to be at the bleeding edge'. They got the job.99

They got the job because they convinced Richard they could create a great web site for a new generation.

● *Chemistry.* It's what I used to call the 'Nottingham Test'. It's
7.30am, Monday, it's raining. Would you want to travel to
Nottingham with this bunch? Chemistry is all.

It's the magic, fizzy stuff that makes them make you make
them perform above your respective games.

And there's no presentational trick whereby you can create it,
except perhaps one – do your research and field the team most
likely to strike a chord (that'll be an intuitive judgement) and
then tell them to be themselves but try to make connections:
points of agreement, disagreement (these may be more
important) and to remember one thing: the audience has to enjoy
this and feel good about themselves. Loved the presentation,
hated the presenters is a lousy start to a business marriage.

2. The contest

Anyone who hasn't done one of these has missed out on one
of life's great, gruesome experiences. It's a cross between
Opportunity Knocks, Mastermind, the first night of a new play,
opening the batting on a lively wicket, and being expert defence
witness with a particularly well-informed and nasty prosecution
barrister.

Here the presentation is key. And to many it is everything to
the extent that the argument and end game are subsumed
beneath a mass of charts, slides, acetates or a fearsome battery of
electronic visual aids.

You've been briefed. You've conducted dozens of interviews,
commissioned expensive research, read hundreds of documents
and reinvented the wheel several times.

All sense of focus has long gone. The Protestant work ethic
has taken over, together with a nasty touch of manic theatricality.

This is showtime and if you have your way, it'll be the full, uncut four-hour *Hamlet*.

You've completely forgotten your audience and their needs except to believe that now they've paid for their tickets, as it were, they'll have to sit through it.

if he were to write a **detective story** it would be called
The Butler Did It

Richard French, one of the great doyens of advertising in the seventies and eighties, someone who had a great 'touch' for the business while recognizing the need for the thick document and the imposing presentation, had, in fact, the attention span of a genius. Namely a few nanoseconds. We truly believed if he were to write a detective story it would be called *The Butler Did It*. He wanted to cut to the chase and used to say:

> If the client came in now – two days before the presentation when, of course, it isn't ready – and said, 'I've got five minutes. Tell me in a nutshell what you're going to tell me in two days' time.' If you can do that, then you may have something good.

Today they call this the 'elevator pitch'. You and the CEO in the lift with perhaps 40 seconds to tell him what you want him to buy.

It's called starting at the end. Identifying the strategic destination and providing a remorseless logic which shows how you got from A to Z, bearing in mind the audience knows all about A and doesn't know a thing about Z which is, hopefully, a promised land.

In the contest a team of presenters who:

- know their stuff
- make the presentation slick, easy to follow and interesting
- are disciples of the 'less is more' school
- all have a role (nothing is ever worse than a bunch of hangers on)
- know where they're going and why they're going there

provide a welcome change to most presentations and they might even win it (if their solution is good enough).

One caveat.

No presentation, however good, can beat the right kind of reconnaissance. It's not uncommon to find yourself presenting to idiots. Unfortunately these idiots own the right to decide whether to give you large sums of money or not. As Orvis, the US leisure goods retail genius, said:

66 The customer's right even when he's godamned wrong. 99

If they are – idiots, that is – you'd better know before the day and prepare accordingly. If you want to win, that is.

If your strategy is to win, knowing your audience is a pretty fundamental starting point. Marketeers who specialize in target marketing too often get diverted by the machismo appeal of contest when involved in a presentation and forget their basic trade.

'Connectivity', a current buzz word, is fundamental to 'contest presentations' and you can't connect if you don't know and understand what you're trying to connect with.

Final point. Look good. Looking good cannot hurt your cause. Make your presentation zing with presentational surprises. It's more fun to deliver. It's a lot more fun to watch.

Make your presentation zing with presentational surprises.

3. Buy this. Now.

This calls for simplicity.

We both know why we're here. As Bernard Shaw said to the simpering lady next to him: 'Madam, would you sleep with me for £1 million?'

She replied: 'Oh Mr Shaw, you are extraordinary'.

He riposted: 'Madam, would you sleep with me for £1?'

She (angrily): 'Mr Shaw, what do you take me for?'

He: 'That, madam, has already been established. We are now merely negotiating the price'.

This is, in short, transaction time. You (Mr Buyer) have a need. I (Mr Seller) have a solution. Let's examine that need to see just how perfectly my solution solves it. QED.

The art of presentation here is in confident simplicity. But it is still an art, weaving a story which leads to the 'buy this, now' end point.

And don't underestimate the buyer. The sales process encapsulated in a well-constructed presentation flatters the buyer and produces – after appropriate negotiation (you each know your walk-away position) – an 'honours satisfied on both sides' situation.

4. The cold canvass big sell

You have an idea. A big one. You're looking for a backer or a sponsor. Millions of pounds are at stake. By definition you won't know your audience very well. By definition they will be more sales resistant than usual. You represent the threat of change, a potential evacuation of their comfort zone. They represent money.

Presenting in such a fraught situation poses its own peculiar problems. You have to establish trust and capture their imagination very quickly. Too cocky and they'll turn off. Too laid back and they'll turn over in their metaphorical 'I'm being presented to' bed.

You have to establish trust and capture their imagination very quickly.

Colin Prescot, CEO of Flying Pictures, the world's largest producer and filmer of aerial stunts, is no stranger to this kind of presentation. His life, told eloquently in his recently published *To The Edge Of Space*, is full of such presentational stories. He flew to Chicago to present to the board of a major multinational and the CEO went to sleep. Twice he made a battery of presentations to discover the sell that was to all intents and purposes 'in the bag' turned out to be a bag of string with rather large holes out of which the contract escaped.

This is where the ability to tell a story with a beginning, middle and end that stays riveted in the minds of its audience is key.

One or two other characteristics are needed, such as good humour, resilience and patience. Such presentations often provoke a 'no' but initially seldom better than a 'maybe' response.

Very often you'll have a champion from within the company who has sponsored this presentation, put their neck on the block, and to see them visibly rooting for you can be as distracting as anything else because you have split loyalties – not to let them down and to get a positive response for your project from their peers.

The cost and style of the presentation should reflect its importance. While great narrative presenters can get away with murder, even they need to recognize a $1 million 'sell' needs to be imbued with a $1 million care and flair.

5. The sting in the tail

This is the matter-of-course, normal presentation with the legitimate request that X or Y is bought at the end of it (although the presentation *per se* isn't, of course, directed to this end but merely provides an excuse for it).

To get what you want, you need:

1. A cogent, logical presentation which underlines at every step:

   - your mastery of the task
   - your complete sense of realism
   - your ability to visualize the future.

2. The ability to get your audience to participate because it's unlikely your 'sting' is going to be part of your formal presentation. Building rapport will be critical to the denouement when, if you manoeuvre it right, they may say: 'That's fine. Oh and is there anything else you want?'

That's when you smile, sit down again, and say 'not really. But…'

'But' is a very powerful word sometimes.

6. Hidden agendas

This, if you buy the thesis about the psychology of buying and selling, is where the response to the question above is:

> No. Not yet. I'll tell you when I do.

It presupposes that you live in an environment where presentations are the norm of your corporate life.

We have strong views that this shouldn't be so, that presentations were, among other things, what did for IBM in the eighties – too many decks of acetates, too much introspection, executives presenting to executives and not focusing on their customers.

Yet if you're a corporate animal you'd better be a great presenter too. It goes with the territory. And if you do have a long-term hidden agenda, plan your presentations half a dozen ahead so they all link together and by the time your audience begins to detect the pattern, they're already well down the road along which, ever so gently, you're leading them.

7. The fishing trip

These call for rare skill. Nigel Clare, former CEO of Heinz Retail Europe, believes these provide the bedrock to the killer presentation yet to come.

❝You have to know what practically can and cannot be done. Formal presentations, by their nature, fall short of asking the unaskable or proposing the 'what would happen if ...' question.

But if you're trying to gain competitive advantage – and you are aren't you, the whole time? – you'd better lay some groundbait and find out how big the fish are or if there are any there at all.❞

This is a world of either no presentation at all or one with such cryptic bullet points you are in total command of the agenda, where it's going and where it might go.

In the more grown-up world of real life this is called 'can I come and have a cup of tea and talk through a few things?'

It may sound odd that a chapter which began by decrying the hard sell appears seamlessly, or perhaps not so seamlessly, to conclude by espousing hard – or hardish – sales presentational techniques.

To achieve anything in business we have to make people do things they either hadn't thought of doing before or which they really hadn't wanted to do until they thought about it again. Much of this is about conditioning audiences so they hear what you have to say – and what's more, want to listen.

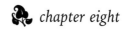

chapter eight

THE FINAL ANALYSIS

Justifying your performance

The most difficult presentation for most of us is Justifying Our Performance.

As a junior executive presenting to your boss or a CEO presenting to financial analysts, your job may not be on the line, but it sure feels that way. And increasingly your job will indeed be on the line. As presentation skills become more and more important in business, if you can't present it then you ain't going to make it.

In just 20 minutes careers and reputations can be ruined, and very publicly. Remember Gerald Ratner, he of the eponymous jewellery chain who famously described a cheap decanter as 'crap'? Something we all knew, something he had said before. But the wrong time and the wrong place, and the press crucified him and his company.

And Peter Job, Chief Executive at Reuters? At the height of market excitement about the potential of the web he failed to present analysts with a convincing case for his Internet plans and his share price plummeted. Only a huge amount of work and another presentation months later, very carefully thought through and impeccably handled, started to restore the reputation of both him and the company.

Even two years later the press still referred to his company as 'signally unskilled at getting its own message across' (*Financial Times*, 7 December 2000).

Journalists have long memories.

The Analyst Presentation – a twice yearly ritual suffered by any public company of any size – is an extreme example of the genre. Justify your performance in front of a critical audience of horribly well-informed analysts with long memories, or die.

As an insurance analyst pointed out to us:

> **66** There is no doubt that a strong presentation can have a significant impact on a company's share price. **99**

It holds useful lessons for anyone at any level.

The agenda is simple enough. Show the numbers. Explain anything out of the ordinary. Convince the audience that you know where you are going, that where you are going is (and remains) sensible, and that you are in control.

That's what you say.

Of course, what you *don't* say can be just as important as what you do say (remember the dog that didn't bark in the Sherlock Holmes' story *Silver Blaze?*).

And **saying too much** can be just as dangerous as **saying too little.**

There's no surer sign of nervous management than swamping the audience with such detail that the overall picture gets lost.

Unless of course you want the overall picture to be lost.

Concentrating on lots of new information in one area is a well-known way of diverting it from another. Well known to analysts, too.

So the first lesson to be learned is to ask yourself why you are giving the presentation, and what it is you want to achieve.

Gauging the audience

At Showcase we work with many large public companies on their presentations to analysts, and we decided we needed to know more about this particular audience. So we commissioned Douglas Miller of Sensus to carry out some research.

Douglas interviewed dozens of market analysts who proved in general to be a busy, forthright bunch with low boredom thresholds.

Why, we wondered, would overworked analysts leave their plush home at 5.30 on a chilly October morning so they could see a CEO and their team make a presentation in the City some three hours later, when everything that was said was available straight to their desktop anyway?

Were these people presentation junkies? Or perhaps too long in the City had merely turned them into masochists.

Well, it became clear that analysts regard watching management live and on the record as an essential part of their job.

66I have never knowingly missed a presentation.99

Insurance analyst

Apart from the facts presented, the team confidence, body language and the way they react to each other are all part of the impression the audience takes away.

66There's definitely a value in seeing the management eyeball to eyeball. You can see whether they're bored or excited, whether they might be lying – that sort of thing.99

Insurance analyst

66You can often tell whether people are telling you rubbish or not from their body language.99

Food analyst

To judge your audience before they begin judging you, start by understanding their needs and expectations.

- Who are they?
- Why are they here?
- What mood are they in?
- Why do they want to listen to *you*?
- How much time have they got?
- What are their like and dislikes?
- Which is more important to them, your presentation or the chance to ask you questions?

Telling the story

Although there is usually a strong emphasis on figures in these presentations, make sure you tell the story behind the numbers. Without an underlying story there is no context and the figures have limited relevance.

Keep moving the story on, don't merely reprise the figures.

> **❝**I would criticize banks for simply reading the chairman's statement to the analysts.**❞**
>
> *Bank analyst*

And don't confuse volume of information with value of information. Volume is much less important than relevance.

So what are you going to say (and what are you *not* going to say?). Develop the structure, perhaps:

- This is what we said we'd do.
- This is what we did.
- These are the results.
- This is how we plan to move on forwards.

What is your one big point, the one you want everyone to take away? Remember that there is no such thing as several big points – they simply become several little ones.

> ## Remember that there is no such thing as several big points – they simply become several little ones.

Now simplify, and don't get mired in detail. Anticipate likely questions and think how best to answer them.

And remember John Cleese in *Fawlty Towers*? – don't mention the war? Don't get fixated on what you must not say.

Simplicity sells

Visuals aids should complement the verbal presentation, not distract attention from it. They should be clear, concise, cohesive and consistent.

Avoid cramming too much detail on to your slides. It is much easier to follow several simple slides than one packed with information. Remember that slides are there to support the speaker, not the other way round.

66 The best companies tend to put up rather less but it's meaningful; the worst are loaded up with unreadable tables. 99

Oil analyst

66 The simpler the better. 99

Food retail analyst

Good visuals convey clear thinking; used well they propel your arguments. Poor visuals simply make you look unprofessional.

Consistency shows stability and confidence

Consistency from one presentation to the next may seem boring and predictable to the presenter, but to a regular audience it is helpful. They interpret 'boring' as consistent, which suggests you have confidence in the method; analysts see your house style perhaps twice a year so they won't get tired of it nearly as quickly as you.

Freshen it up from time to time by all means, but be cautious about wholesale changes. Predictable means that nothing is amiss, no alarm bells start flashing. Consistency makes comparisons easier. Changes in structure or definition mean that comparisons become tenuous which in turn creates frustrated analysts or – worse – wrong inferences to be drawn.

66 Occasionally companies decide to change the format ... usually it's to hide something that's gone wrong. 99

Food analyst

Be consistent. It shows coherency, stability and confidence. Unexplained change may suggest unexplained problems.

This is business, not theatre

Good visuals can help make a good presentation, but the star of the show is the speaker, not the graphics. A chief executive told us that he was 'merely the servant of the company', 'that the visual aids and handouts are what matters'.

But he is wrong – people are much more interesting to an audience than the graphics and the management stands there, warts and all, on the record and accountable. Graphics are there simply to help the speaker and the audience communicate.

The best graphics pin down key issues, helping you look good and appear clear and thoughtful.

Beware of too much theatre, especially of the high-tech variety. Analysts are suspicious of 'the sell', and of inappropriate displays of high technology.

66Where there's too much hype you're not believed. The message doesn't get through at all.99

Pharmaceutical analyst

But for all that, visuals remain important. The standard in London, for example, is high.

you drop below an acceptable local standard at your peril

66You have in the UK a pretty high standard. You cannot afford not to conform to it if you want to be taken seriously.99

Media analyst

Appearance is reality

There's more to it than just the visuals. Poor organization, a disjointed presentation or a bad team performance create an adverse impression of a company and its management.

66I think the manner of the presentation is a reflection of where the business is, or where the management feel they've got to.99

Food retailers analyst

Or, more basically:

66Just make sure it all works ...99

General retailers analyst

Rehearse your speech (but not too much). Talk it through out loud.

Does it still fit the time you've got? Rehearse your team. Rehearse your equipment.

Look confident; many good presenters are nervous (join the gang). Remind yourself that you know more about your subject than your audience. Remember that it is *you* they want to see.

What you see is what you get

Then there's the handout – now virtually obligatory, and increasingly in colour. The packs should be available at the start and contain every slide (ideally on a white background so that notes can be made on them).

Add non-essential information as notes or appendices. This helps reduce the amount of extraneous information that appears during the presentation itself.

> ❝They add additional information which is very useful because it means you don't have to take as many notes.❞
>
> *Food retailers analyst*

Handouts are a useful *aide-mémoire*, useful for notes made during the presentation, and if all else fails, an invariably useful backup.

Face values

For those who can't present to all their audience in person, web and video conferencing are becoming more common, especially for minor announcements or where long-distance travel would be a poor investment of time or money.

These are a poor substitute for live meetings and

they add a layer of technological risk and remoteness

but the presence of an audience who would otherwise have no chance to join in the process may be compensation enough.

Web-casting presentations – recording the presentation on video and making it available on a web site either live or after a short delay – can be a useful adjunct to presentations particularly if supporting data is included, such as the text of the speech, the numbers in spreadsheet form, the slides, etc.; but it is still no substitute for a live show.

None of these technologies will diminish the pre-eminence of face-to-face meetings.

The analyst who insisted:

66 I will always want to see the whites of their eyes 99

captured the feelings of all audiences everywhere.

INSPIRERS, PERSPIRERS, ASPIRERS

part two

❧

Interviews with master presenters

Your move, Mike

Mike Kirsch, Consumer Business Director, Norwich Union Life

❧

The exam technique

Chris Pinnington, Managing Director of Euro RSCG Wnek Gosper

❧

Movers, shakers and mega deal makers

Lucas van Praag, a Managing Director at Goldman Sachs, London

❧

The triumph of deep knowledge over style

Simon Skeldon, Client Services Director, Taylor Nelson Sofres

❧

The stamp of authority

Dr Neville Bain, Chairman, Consignia (formerly The Post Office)

❧

The devastating silence of an entrepreneur

Michael Ullmann, Adjunct Professor of Entrepreneurship, INSEAD

❧

Schooled in business

Marcus Alexander, Adjunct Professor, London Business School

Mike Kirsch
Your move, Mike

Mike Kirsch, unlike the exotic drink after which he is named, has his feet soberly on the ground. More real ale than cocktail. He exudes self-belief and a belief in the ideals of his customers.

He's Consumer Business Director of Norwich Union Life, with 5,500 people reporting to him (good luck Mike, that's a regiment or three). He's responsible for Your Move – the estate agency arm – healthcare and the direct channels of NU.

He was breathless when I called, having rushed in from a meeting:

66 I've only got ten minutes. 99

Amazing what adrenalin can produce in ten minutes when laser-type questions drill into your brain.

He does lots of presentations. He loves doing them. No equivocation here – just loves them.

66 They give me an opportunity to perform. Yes, I admit I like that, I like taking the airwaves – and sharing my thoughts with people and sometimes (and this is great) actually influencing them, their behaviour and events in the future of the company. 99

The most difficult thing, he believes, in all presentations is 'pitching it right'. In any meeting, for instance, understanding the various agendas people have is key. Thinking it through from their point of view is a must.

Mike talks about hitting the 'hot buttons'. Without research or diligent reconnaissance, however good the slides look is irrelevant.

66 Presentations, like ads, need careful targeting. 99

I asked him how much better he'd got over the years. Now, imagine Mike (he'll kill me for this) – slightly overweight, nearing 40, energy levels to die for (most would have done so by now at his pace of life), hobby: catching 40lb carp, mostly in France.

I've known him since he was a junior marketing manager. He was good then. Today he can – on form – inspire. I've seen him on form.

Every time you think you've got better, the audience goes up a notch.

The presentation game is full of banana skins.

66 **Don't ever, ever get complacent about it.** 99

He distinguishes more simply than some between the inspirational and the sales presentation.

66 **Showpiece presentations like annual sales conferences are high risk because your performance is visible to a much wider audience than you can normally influence … they are one-off events and tend to linger in the memory longer.** 99

Performance is as important as content. You can do a good presentation with limited content. But good content weakly delivered will never be seen as a good presentation.

He defines the art of mass communication:

66 **It's about getting the tone right and hitting the hot buttons a few times.** 99

The sales presentation is more complex and involves more tangible issues (do you make that sale in the end?).

Lessons:

1. Keep it simple.
2. Be clear what you're saying.
3. Talk to the lowest common denominator.
4. Understand what they want.

Mike, as an inveterate coarse fisherman, understands better than most the need to be patient but also to understand if the fish are feeding in a desultory or purposeful way. He fashions his presentations accordingly.

The world has changed, he concedes.

❝There are more ways of presenting nowadays which means more opportunities for technology to get you.

Computer presentations are more temperamental than my wife.❞

But small groups are fun, he says, where you can 'exploit' – eye contact, the names of the people, anecdotes about them, a whole series of ways of engaging them as people, not employees or peers.

Bad presentations comprise:

- slides you can't read
- fantastic graphics but 'what's he saying?'
- smart arses.

Mike is eloquent, incandescent even, about intellectual arrogance, about presenters who take an 'up yours' stance to the bottom quartile of their audience, especially in a sales conference.

❝If they can't or won't present properly to us, how can they expect us to do a convincing sales job to an ordinary customer?❞

Best presentations – just one example.
Churchill.

His one-line presentation (Mike couldn't remember to whom and nor could I):

66 **Never, never, never give up.** 99

Few, powerful words are what impress, plus, of course, oodles of enthusiasm and energy.

What are powerful words?

66 **Words which are simple, everyday, concrete words, words delivered with passion.** 99

Any advice?

66 **Never be afraid to seek help because how you present yourself matters a lot.** 99

how you present yourself matters a lot

Chris Pinnington
The exam technique

Chris Pinnington is Managing Director of Euro RSCG Wnek Gosper, the tenth largest UK advertising agency with 200 employees and part of the Havas Group, the fifth largest communications group in the world.

I used to work with Chris and recall his obsession with focus and simplicity in presentations. He belongs more to the Samuel Beckett than the Shakespearean school of presenters. But, as results show, he is extremely successful at it.

the best presenters exude true brilliance with no apparent time spent on rehearsal

He says presentations are like exams. While the best presenters exude true brilliance with no apparent time spent on rehearsal, the reality is that impeccable and extensive homework is required.

66 **Remember the audience's point of view. You look completely different to how you think you look, so rehearse in front of a video camera which nowadays is really easy to do.** 99

Presenters are made, not born (and the few who are born are very lucky indeed). There's no substitute for practising in front of your peers and there's little that is as frightening.

Learn to be your own person. Don't try to work to a formula. Be big enough to recognize the value of professional training, but use a coach who draws performance out of you rather than one who rams it in.

However, Chris, like many others who daily present for their very careers, is uneasy about the over-coached presenter. He recalls a slick Michael Portillo at a Marketing Society lunch.

"He was just too polished, too glib, and frankly lost credibility by his stuck-on 'I am sincerely presenting to you' persona."

Chris has a series of tips which he passes down to his own people.

1. Memorize and make as memorable as you can the first point of the presentation. Remember, it's hard to recover from a rocky start. Most of us will recall his own greatest fear:

"the propensity to blush and wish you could get out of there."

2. Always plan exit points so that the presentation that goes awry (and however much you plan this can still happen) can be allowed to end apparently naturally as opposed to precipitately. Sometimes, he notes, clients simply run out of time. Don't trap them in a never-ending presentation.

3. Minimize the number of charts – all too often they distract audiences. Chris believes the audience should look at the presenter.

"It's *your* eyes that count."

Look at your audience. It also helps you see what they're thinking.

4. Remember what clients respond to. Often, simply, it's down to:

"Do I like this person?"

Content comes second to giving yourself time and space to engage them and be likeable.

5. Avoid humour. Stand-up comedians tend not to be good salespeople.

(I recall as he says this the late Mike Pullman, one of London's leading advertising copywriters and a wonderfully funny man, saying to me 30 years ago: 'No one buys something important from a clown.'

No one buys something important from a clown.

thereby firing an exocet into the often claimed view of advertising people that funny commercials sell best.)

6. Be you. Not a presentation machine.

7. Invite audience response. Everyone likes the sound of their own voice more than yours.

Chris recalls his two worst presentation experiences.

Australia. The late eighties. Presenting to Alan Bond for the Hyundai Car account. The essence of this was to prove that Hyundai was made from strong steel while ordinary Japanese cars were made from poor, tinny material.

To prove this point with some drama the agency set up a side-by-side comparison. Two car bonnets placed in the boardroom. Enter a well-known Korean kick boxer who by attacking each would prove conclusively that Hyundai was the stronger.

All looked good until the kick boxer's frenzied attack on the Japanese bonnet impelled it against the fine mahogany door of the boardroom, splintering it irreparably.

The presentation ended just about as it began, with Alan Bond suggesting (I'm not sure if I took this down right) that they 'kick off'.

The second, a classic issue of context, was when the beguiling Jacques Seguela (the 'S' in 'RSCG'), presenting to a client in Salt Lake City, espoused the need for passion. He spoke eloquently and said what only a Frenchman would do.

66 **Passion is vital. You want people around you who do a lot of fucking.** 99

Not in Salt Lake City you don't, Jacques. Not with all those Mormons around. Language, *mon brave*.

The best presenter Chris has seen is Bob Schmetterer, who spends a fortune on speechwriters, props, autocues – the whole works. And it works.

❝It isn't slick. It's just terrific. Very engaging. Clearly well prepared, thought through.

He makes *you* feel good.

He makes *you* feel important because he's obviously attached so much importance to it.❞

> He makes *you* feel
> important because he's obviously
> attached so much importance to it.

What's changed?

In the mid-eighties a hugely successful agency called Allen Brady & Marsh mounted extravaganza showtime presentations. They made Busby Berkeley look like a provincial repertory tap dance routine artist. Sums well over £100,000 were spent on a single presentation – probably more than £350,000 in today's money.

❝Clients hate this nowadays. They want to see chemistry, thinking, content. You spend a much smaller sum.❞

PowerPoint has taken over (you can almost produce a presentation as they're coming up in the lift), but it is 'beauty and the beast'. Most people overchart and create what Chris calls 'chart blindness'. Some of the best presentations he's done, he says, have been chartless.

CHRIS PINNINGTON

Some of the best presentations he's done, he says, have been chartless.

Chartless and artless seems to be the message.

> **In the end people want to hear you talk, not lecture.**
>
> **In the end they want to know if they can work *with* you.**
>
> **A great, staged presentation can never really tell them that.**

Lucas van Praag
Movers, shakers and mega deal makers

Lucas van Praag joined the Merchant Navy when he left school. He learned his presentation skills as a midshipman.

66This was mainly telling people what to do ... I soon realized that this was only the first part of the process. Making sure something happened was the next. That was a good lesson.99

Lucas is now a Managing Director at Goldman Sachs, the investment bank, in London.

At their best, he feels, presentations distil ideas into an easily digested form. So by their very existence presentations comprise an intellectual discipline. It seems to take many people a long time to discover this.

presentations distil ideas into
an easily digested form

He believes you should engage with the people you are presenting to, find ways of interacting or challenging their assumptions. This is what makes presenting enjoyable and exciting. He likes nothing better than interruptions from his audience.

66Lack of response means you're doing it wrong. When there's no chemistry and no response from your audience, you have an uphill struggle.99

Inevitably you've got to have words in your slides. But pictures tend to be much more useful and much more flexible even than video.

Newspaper cuttings are very effective because they simplify and dramatize issues.

66 **Anything that's fast, contemporary and easy to absorb works brilliantly.** 99

Lucas believes that you can either talk to the general concept of a slide or you can talk to the detailed bullet points. But good presenters often avoid talking too much detail.

He makes a shrewd assessment of the British versus American presentation cultures:

66 **American business values are at the heart of PowerPoint. The British 'old school tie' approach is essentially anti-presentation.** 99

At Goldman Sachs, home to American business values if ever there was one, presentations matter.

66 **Internal and external presentations are part of our lifeblood. We use them to communicate change internally, and externally they are a compelling mechanism for presenting our ideas and views.** 99

Within Goldman Sachs' various offices in Europe there are 89 different nationalities. So even though it is a homogenous group corporately, there is huge variety in terms of culture and background.

Lucas describes the Goldman Sachs culture and how presentations fit in.

66 **We have many people here working on a wide variety of topics, from advisory projects to thought leadership, so presenting, and being presented to, are daily events.** 99

He reflects on national diversity:

66 Some people believe that the French over-communicate. As a nation of thinkers they seem to believe that more words equals more thought. This can lead to mental indigestion for the audience. 99

they seem to believe that more words equals more thought

(Perhaps this could be described as 'More = More'.)

66 The British minimalist school is equally problematic. The one-word bullet that is so enigmatic only the speaker understands the meaning, and anybody reading the presentation afterwards can make neither head nor tail of it. This sometimes includes the speaker. 99

('Less = More'.)

66 The Americans imbibe presentation skills with their mothers' milk, they tend to be very focused on what they *say*, paying less attention to their visuals. 99

(One of the few to praise American presenters. God bless Lucas. God bless America.)

66 Italians can be very similar to the French, and revel in the continental trait of using entire paragraphs as headings.

Germans are generally less verbose than the French. They are usually better at editing their material but can end up simply stating the obvious. 99

Lucas worked in South Africa on the Sanlam demutualization, a major event in the country's business development. Many of the target audience couldn't read, so they used an industrial theatre troop to tour the country, dramatizing the issues and explaining the options.

66Maybe even the sophisticated presentational world of PowerPoint and multimedia interactive shows distributed on the web has something to learn from going back to grass roots.99

He lays out the disasters that can happen to everyone in the inevitable rush to put together a presentation:

- Spelling the name of a company wrong. How can this ever happen? But it is so obvious that it is easily overlooked.

- Using the wrong logo. All too easy when you try to find a logo on the web – it may be out of date or the operator may simply have selected the wrong 'Smith'.

- Using a codename instead of the company name. Simply forgetting at the last moment is all too easy when you've used the codename for weeks – it is so familiar and everybody is dog-tired.

- Using an old presentation but updating it improperly. Lots of ways of doing this, from using 'find and replace' without concentrating hard on the result to picking the wrong presentation as the base.

- Misinterpreting the brief. All too easy. Like exams. Once you have got up a head of steam it is very hard to go back and look clear-sightedly at the brief.

- Failing to realize that the audience doesn't want a presentation but wants to talk. Ah, yes ...

- A technical breakdown. Understandable but unforgivable, especially if you've no backup.

the bigger the team, the less the individual responsibility and so the more likely mistakes are to happen

But not everything ends in tears. He tells the story of a former colleague, Karen Simmons, who once arranged a presentation for City analysts. With the audience assembled and the presentation ready to start, nothing worked. Disaster. Unabashed, Karen announced that everybody should go outside where she would find taxis and the presentation would proceed back at her office.

But when they got outside it was pouring with rain and inevitably there were no taxis. At this point most people would have given up, thinking the gods were against them. But Karen saw an empty coach heading towards her, stepped out in front of it, forced it to stop and did a cash deal with the driver.

66 **The presentation went ahead, her reputation was made and she has never looked back.** 99

I asked Lucas what represented success. He thought for a few minutes, then said wryly:

66 **What makes a presentation a triumph? Thorough planning, a receptive audience – and no screw-ups!** 99

And to summarise:

66 **Engaging the audience is what makes it work, makes it memorable and achieves the result.** 99

Presentations are about people, not about process.

Simon Skeldon
The triumph of deep knowledge over style

Simon Skeldon is Client Services Director of Taylor Nelson Sofres, Europe's most powerful research company. We saw Simon dazzling an audience at an Organic Foods Conference, hence this interview.

He believes the use of language is very important, that jargon is a form of tribalization and creates high barriers to entry. Taylor Nelson needs to put numbers into context, often with comparable data. This can result in detailed charts, so Simon eschews the 'less is more argument', saying it is irrelevant to his demands.

The 'less is more' argument, is irrelevant to my demands.

He prefers to issue the handouts after the presentation to keep people's attention on what he's saying. If you are teeing people up for the climax, you don't want them racing ahead.

He's a think-on-your-feet interactor:

66 It's important to be flexible, to see the audience's reaction to a chart and then work with that reaction. 99

But being a good researcher, he's more research than presentation focused and *always* goes back to the data.

Automatic charting can be dangerous. Anything which stops people digging around in the data he regards as dangerous.

66 There is always a balance to be drawn between style and content. You have got to get the content right. It is much better to listen to somebody with bad charts but first-rate knowledge than the other way around. 99

When Taylor Nelson trains new graduates it insists on the primacy of the content. Style can come later.

❝I recently attended a fascinating conference. Sir Peter Davies spoke on IT but it was clear that he was not on his own subject.

Procter & Gamble had video, music, the full monty, but it all went wrong. Not their fault.

Carlos Criado-Perez from Safeway had no slides. He spoke exactly to time. He was impeccably dressed and impeccably mannered. Completely professional and very, very good.

Tim Mason and the marketing team from Tesco rolled up their sleeves.

Allan Leighton took off his jacket, walked around, frequently turned his back on the audience, but was very engaging.❞

It takes all types.

Simon does 70–100 presentations a year. He tends to rough them out and his support team will fill in the details. He presents to clients, at internal presentations and at a number of conferences.

Presentations are just one way in which he communicates. He sends out databases to clients and produces reports. But presentations are the way to get key facts to key people. Here's the question you asked us, here's the answer, and this is what makes the answer significant.

Presentations are the way to get key facts to key people.

❝Style depends very much on the platform. At a conference you have to look professional. With a client, sometimes the back of an envelope can be more engaging.❞

Although he stresses again and again the importance of content over style, it is, he believes, essential that the numbers are *accessible* to the audience and the means of delivery must not misrepresent them. At the end of the day, clients know much more about their products or brands than you do.

66 **The biggest change is in using computers directly rather than OHPs. The purpose of the presentation has not changed. What has changed is the immediacy. It is quicker. And we can do more with it.**

Ten years ago it might take two weeks to process the data and chart it. Now it takes half an hour. *But ten years ago we knew the data in much more depth*.

In ten years' time retailers and brand owners will have direct access to consumers and will be able to draw down vast amounts of data. However, they will not necessarily have the corresponding skills to interpret it. 99

Simon is good at what he does and deeply serious about it. However, he tells the story with some relish of a colleague he once saw

66 **sort a set of overheads into two piles – the pile he wanted for a major presentation and the pile of rejects. Unfortunately, as he left the office he picked up the wrong pile, which he only discovered when he began the presentation. The presentation went fine and the client had no idea of the problem. This is an example of the triumph of deep knowledge over style.** 99

the **triumph** of
deep knowledge **over style**

He then tells the story of President Bill Clinton in his first speech to the Senate.

66 **He decided to use autocue so there was no need for notes. When he walked up to the podium the autocue was dead. Every presenter's worst nightmare. He spoke beautifully and finished exactly on time.** 99

He summarizes the real art of presenting:

66 **So what you need to be a great presenter is flexibility, the ability to think while presenting and to react to the audience.** 99

Sounds easy, doesn't it? But if you're dealing with the masses of data Simon's handling, presentations probably seem a little less consequential than calculus. And he worries more about the content – what the presentation actually says – than the way it looks. A supporter of deep knowledge rather than style.

Dr Neville Bain
The stamp of authority

Dr Neville Bain is Chairman of Consignia (formerly the Post Office) and author of a number of business books on general management, corporate governance, and the way businesses use and develop their people.

An experienced presenter, more than anyone I have met he can listen to a question, organize his thoughts and rattle off a thoughtful, coherent and complex answer at a galloping pace.

"Presentations are primarily about the ability to influence."

He is a passionate exponent of the power of presentations: And the importance of communication in general:

66 The role of communications overall has to be understood. It's hugely important for people to understand the framework they are working in, and recognize in turn how their own troops see them.

That's why communication is so important. And presentations are a key part of this. 99

The basic question you must always ask when developing a presentation is:

"What is this doing to get my message across?"

Neville works directly on his own presentations.

❝I work directly on to PowerPoint. My first cut of slides is for establishing ideas and structure. My second cut refines and simplifies.❞

Note the 'simplifies'. So many of our interviewees come back to this critical process of honing and simplifying.

❝It's essential to be analytical to get the structure right.❞

Neville is, by his own admission, a very structured person. He plans every presentation to these four points:

● What is the key message?

● How best can I get it across?

● How can I create a logical construction?

● How can I drive that logic to only one possible conclusion?

He believes that

every presentation should have a
strong beginning and a strong ending

Some of his rules for presentations are:

1. Make sure each slide is punchy, has impact, and is not too wordy.

2. Delivering it must add point to the presentation and drive it forward.

3. Shorter is better than longer.

4. The classic presentational layout is:
—topic (i.e. the key message)
—agenda
—presentation

—key message (again)

—conclusion.

He likes to get away from an over-reliance on bullet points and headlines.

❝I use graphics and video extensively.❞

He reflects on what audiences expect and respond to. Understanding their expectations is key. The political arena is no exception.

❝Ministers tend to be suspicious of over-professional presentations, so I often use just hard copy. I must give them something to take away; private secretaries take briefing notes anyway.❞

He is withering in his criticism of bad presentations, two sorts in particular:

1. The poor, unintelligible, badly structured presentation, usually with lots of visual aids, often in a loose-leaf folder. Many gurus use this method. It's often entertaining, even fascinating, and its masters can give a great performance; but it's not good practice and certainly not well structured and effective as communication.

2. The technology-led (usually PowerPoint) presentation. These often tend to be

full of whizz-bangs that add nothing to the sum total of human knowledge

Nor does he favour technological aids such as autocue.

❝I hate it. I like notes in the form of bullets for speaking from. I let myself be scripted only reluctantly.❞

Neville trained at Cadbury. He recognized early on that presentational competence mattered. On an early training video he felt he came across as a 'fervent Presbyterian minister' with photochromic spectacles that made him look like a member of the Mafia. So he worked on body language and expressions to find a more positive presentation persona. And now uses clear glasses for presentations.

But he's not keen on too much formal training, although Consignia provides courses. He prefers now to act as mentor, to offer guidance and advice.

He used to run Coats Viyella, the textiles company. He remembers a major international management conference where the IT department wanted to increase its credibility and influence and decided to strut its stuff – with presentations from all over the world coordinated and assembled at the last minute.

But sadly, one had a virus which infected all the others.

The IT team tried to rescue the situation and recreate everything from scratch but ran out of time. As a result they ended up with nothing. There was no fallback position.

A sad and perhaps not uncommon story. However, in this case it destroyed the department's credibility and delayed for months their ability to make their proper contribution. So everyone suffered the consequences.

❝As with everything in life you have to deliver. It's simply not worth putting anything to chance.❞

Presentations really do matter.

Michael Ullmann
The devastating silence of an entrepreneur

Michael Ullmann is charismatic. And restless. And likely to get very exercised by what he sees as sloppy thinking. When he stares at you, you know you've been stared at. He made one of his fortunes in burger buns, so he can't be all bad.

Michael is Adjunct Professor of Entrepreneurship at INSEAD, one of the world's leading business schools. He has taught there for over ten years while continuing to be a successful entrepreneur himself.

He straddles both business and academe with success and evident enjoyment.

At INSEAD he sees a lot of student presentations and says the standards tend to be high.

66 **A really good presentation can transform a mediocre written plan. Personal style becomes much more important than graphics. But the quality of graphics is generally good and you can't get away with weak graphics on a big screen.** 99

A really **good presentation** can transform
a mediocre written plan.

Are there any signs of a new style of presentation emerging from this articulate, computer-literate group?

66 **There's been no sea change. But what is clear is that electronic presentations can be structured better and with more subtlety; point can be superimposed on point to build up a convincing argument. This does require the presenter to give more thought to the process, but that's no bad thing.**

The old-style slide that tries to do everything at once is well past its sell-by date. 🙶

Michael makes the point that cold, hard analysis is only one aspect of business. Passion and involvement and energy are all important ingredients and can be at least as important in a presentation as impeccable charts and innumerable facts.

He asserts (and Michael asserts quite strongly when he asserts) that a presentation should be a call to action or to change a point of view.

🙶**Every presenter must find a balance between *process* and *content*. People focus on content, but the process of communication, how you deliver that content, is very important.** 🙶

There is a continuum from the cold presentation where the audience knows nothing to a presentation that is part of a continuing process with an audience you know. These require different techniques.

🙶**With the first group you have to get their attention very quickly. It is a cold sell and if you haven't made a connection in the first five minutes, you've blown it. With the second you're already past that stage and there isn't the initial pressure; plus the audience has a reason to be there. So you can relax and enjoy yourself.** 🙶

But it's strange isn't it, he ponders, how nervous people get before giving a presentation. Instead of confronting the problem, analyzing it and resolving it, they speak too fast, they twitch, they give all sorts of clues to their feelings. And that can be dangerous. It's distracting. And it can focus the audience on your problems, not your presentation.

So how do you do it, Michael?

Walk in purposefully.
First impressions are important.

66 Walk in purposefully. First impressions are important. Make it work for *you*.

Don't get locked behind the lectern – find the space where you feel comfortable and use it. Move around in it, expand it – keep the focus on yourself by movement.

There are many tricks to get and keep attention. Lowering the tone of your voice. Silent pauses – three seconds of silence takes you outside the normal conversational range and is disturbing; 20 seconds is devastating, nobody knows what's going on. Only you. 99

20 seconds is devastating, nobody knows what's going on. Only you.

Handouts, he feels, are rarely thought through properly and need more attention. There is little awareness of how they can be used to add more value to the presentation except to say 'I've done the work – this proves it'.

66 Formal presentations are needed when approaching institutions about funding or support or taking over a business. Informal ones to staff do not always need visuals and are often all the better for not having them. Salespeople tend to use hard copy presentations – a full audio-visual presentation would be over the top for a one-on-one meeting. 99

Presentations have improved noticeably over the last ten years. People are more competent and confident in using media. Software is easier to use and much more powerful. Things that result in higher production values such as transitions and builds are better used.

Simple things are important, such as highlighting the structure of the presentation – and referring back to it from time to time so that the audience know where they are.

The environment for presentations is much better. Many institutions and companies now have very adequate resources.

66 **Bigger screens, better resolution, better projection all mean that charts are easier to read and clearer. However, people still talk too much to their slides, repeating the points one by one as they appear on the slide. They are much too literal.** 99

There are not enough graphics or pictures. Not enough using pictures to add texture to a presentation – instead of showing head-and-shoulders shots of chief executives, show them with their family or favourite car, something that develops interest in them as a person, as a real human being.

And something Michael feels strongly about, rebelling against the wrong kind of touchy, feely stuff so predominant today.

Differentiate between the *conceptual* and **the *concrete*.**

66 **The concrete can be illustrated and made real. It is too often treated in the same abstract way as the conceptual.** 99

In front of a blazing log fire in his Buckinghamshire home, Michael ponders his worst experience in a presentation.

66 **Somebody falling asleep after too good a lunch. I still haven't worked out how to deal with that one.** 99

Marcus Alexander
Schooled in business

Professor Marcus Alexander is an Adjunct Professor at the London Business School and a Director of the Ashridge Strategic Management Centre. His former headmaster at Westminster, John Rae, told me he was 'one of the most outstanding pupils he'd ever had'. He exudes charm and competence. He is effortlessly effective. It's all pretty hard for mortals like us to take.

Marcus was intrigued by the subject and started by reflecting that nearly all of us are guilty of 'failing to vary what we do presentationally in relation to the context of a presentation'.

He then dissected the presentation with the forensic ease of a classics scholar.

First of all, 'mode of presentation'. Four types he reckons:

1. Is this about *content give out*?

2. Is it about *clarifying content*?

3. Is it about *discussing content*?

4. Is it about *creating content*?

Do the **wrong** presentation and you **confuse** and **frustrate** your audience.

Secondly, numbers and setting. Obviously one-to-one or one-to-two is very different to one-to-many.

66 It's like sport. You're in charge. Decide on the game plan. 99

Marcus is fascinated by locating the 'energy source'. A typical business school presenter exudes high-voltage stuff to keep his audience awake but he recognizes that energy alone is not enough.

❝There's a real danger when I'm tired of simply being energetic, of lacking focus and going nowhere but going there in a frenzy.❞

He identifies:

1. The use of expectancy – much like a comedian uses when he leads protractedly to a punch line (the Tony O'Reilly technique).

2. The use of intellectual energy – not giving away too much, guiding an audience and making *them* work.

3. Basic involvement which, expressed at its simplest, is a conversation.

4. Resistance. Enormously powerful. When the presenter is selling something in the teeth of what the audience actually believes. Hello Devil. Hello Advocate.

He defines his own tree of materials.

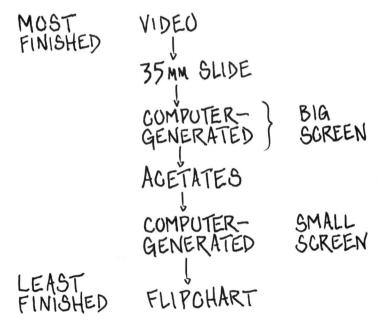

MOST FINISHED

VIDEO
↓
35 MM SLIDE
↓
COMPUTER–GENERATED } BIG SCREEN
↓
ACETATES
↓
COMPUTER–GENERATED   SMALL SCREEN
↓
FLIPCHART

LEAST FINISHED

and he concludes, from his perspective:

MARCUS ALEXANDER

66 Over the years I've come to think I often want to give the feeling my presentation isn't too finished. This allows the audience to participate more. 99

On content he describes various approaches:

- create a logical structure
- tell a story
- illustrate with vignettes
- illustrate with personal experiences.

And he concludes that, at the line manager level, it is the personal experience that most often goes down well.

But unless we decide what the *context* of a presentation is, we're playing blind poker. Hard as it may be to change tempo and style, we must, must do it.

All too often we retreat into non personal presentation mode as a safety device. If we're smart, we're always looking for audience triggers.

This goes as far as what you look like.

66 I think a lot about what I wear, about the room, about whether I'll move around a lot, about how much interaction I want. 99

The worst presentations?
Those where humour is misapplied.

The worst presentations? Those where humour is misapplied. Marcus once went to a Quality Awards presentation where a rather dull man told endless unfunny jokes. Haven't we all done it? Beware. Marcus confessed that he had too. He still cringes at the memory.

An 86-slide presentation from a German CFO.

Presentation Masters

I f you could put a presentational dream team together who between them covered most of the ground of business presentations, it might go something like this:

- a couple of front-line business leaders who've made their reputations by not only devising outstanding strategies but have been able to articulate their ideas and carry audiences with them;
- a pair of leading advisors who deeply understand the impact of presentations on key audiences and specialize in developing and honing the details of the presentation to ensure that all of the right, and none of the wrong, messages come through;
- two top PR people with long experience of judging the wider impact of what you say, and bringing it to the widest possible audience under the most favourable circumstances;
- a brilliant group of designers and operators to get it all together.

So here they are – six of the very best (modesty precludes inclusion of the last members of the team from further comment).

Marjorie Scardino of *Pearson* and **Mike Grabiner** who built up *Energis* – both high profile leaders of fast-growing companies with a consistent track record of success. Both have had to build and argue their cases internally, and present again and again externally to convince an initially sceptical and unresponsive market. They have consistently delivered on their promises and in just a few years have both grown from minor players to major UK business figures.

Lucy Parker of *Trinity Management Communications* and **Howard Coates** of *Makinson Cowell* are two advisors in the thick of every corporate battle, helping refine the explanation of strategy, focus arguments, and find ways of helping over-excited and often over-tired executives express themselves clearly, succinctly and convincingly.

Tony Carlisle of *Citigate Dewe Rogerson* and **Alan Parker** of *Brunswick* have had a huge influence on the public face of corporate reporting during the past decade, in the process turning what was a backwater of the public relations industry into a major, influential and indispensable adjunct to any corporate activity.

Marjorie Scardino

> 66 **In 1996 Marjorie was unknown. She has presented her way to the top.** 99

This strong-minded but softly spoken Texan has in short order taken Pearson from a ragbag conglomerate of leisure, publishing and banking companies to a major player in the high-growth markets of business and educational publishing – online and off. And she has taken the City with her, as her reputation shows.

She has done this with a personal style that is calm, measured, caring and trusting. A colleague describes her as at peace with herself and entirely free of ego. She asks for and takes advice – which means that anyone who works for her knows that what they say really is on the line. And she has created a company that is regarded as one of the most desirable in the world to work for; and an informal environment of mutual respect and downright fun. She is living proof that dynamic management can make a real difference, not just to the bottom line but to the very culture of a company.

Her presentations are characterized by great attention to detail, intense preparation and focus (though usually at a very late stage) and by relaxed delivery and a personal tone of voice.

She is living proof that dynamic management can make a real difference.

 Presentations are important; they force you to get your thinking in order. They take an enormous amount of preparation. You've got to be able to reduce complexity down to simple core ideas.

She likes to use a script, but by the time she comes to speak it is usually so heavily annotated that nobody else could possibly deliver it. The word 'illegible' comes to mind.

I started life as a journalist, so taking a script and editing it is second nature to me. I'm often still working on a script until just before I get up to speak. But when I get there, I do stick to it.

She often starts her presentations informally, standing (shoes often kicked off) at the lectern and simply chatting with the audience. She is very good at establishing the right atmosphere with a few choice remarks.

I like to know my audience. It's a great comfort to know the people you are talking to.

She talks of the importance of setting the agenda for the presentation:

The agenda isn't so much a list of events; it is really a measure of how people are thinking, strategically or whatever.

As the representative of a major media group, Marjorie has built a team of advisors who develop the detail of style and content; again she will take a great deal of advice but at the end of the day it is very much her decision what goes. She is demanding about quality, about accuracy, and about context.

Live presentations are, and will remain, a critical management tool. At their best, presentations enhance understanding, but they also ensure accountability and transparency. They put a premium on strategy and ideas.

And she likes emotion. She wants her audience to feel and think and get excited. While everything is grounded in fact, she likes emotion and feelings and enthusiasm to show. Headlines are active, bullet points are pared away to strong bold statements, and pictures and imagery predominate.

> ❝ How you present is just as important as what you present and computers now let you do so much more in terms of emotion and activity. These days there must be some degree of entertainment value in everything you do. ❞

But visual aids aren't everything.

> ❝ At conferences you can do a lot without slides – ideas, attitudes, atmospherics all play a part. Often the CEO doesn't need slides, especially when you are trying to react to events and achievements: in that context a speech with pre-prepared slides would be quite wrong. ❞

She adds:

> ❝ People should be themselves in presentations, but it does no harm to try to appear in the best possible light. I've now had a lot of practice. But I've also had a lot of support from my husband and that's been important too. ❞

She evidently enjoys the cut and thrust of questions, often coming out from behind the lectern and appearing comfortable simply standing out on the stage talking directly to her audience.

> ❝ I don't do much by way of thinking of all the questions they might ask and preparing answers. I do spend a lot of time thinking about the key themes, how they link together and the best way of explaining them. As a team we think through the issues very carefully and when we answer we are, I think, coherent. I think that's much more important than giving them the right spin. ❞

Mike Grabiner

Mike arrived at *Energis* in 1996. He built the company into a major European telecoms player with a string of acquisitions and one of the fastest sustained growth rates in recent history.

Initially shielded by the bulk of its parent, National Grid, this small stripling of a business, buzzing with energy, has entered the FTSE 100 in its own right, outstripping its parent in the process. We spoke shortly before he announced his departure.

 I spend more time presenting than any other single business activity.

 Communication – not just one way but two – is increasingly important. We need to communicate constantly. Not just with our stakeholders – investors, customers and staff – but also with regulators and suppliers.

Presentations are an essential part of this; and one of the things to remember about presentations is their role in provoking – and giving structure to – discussion.

He prefers a script and usually sticks rigorously to it, but if time is tight he may decide to skip a section on the spur of the moment. This can make for an exciting time for the computer operator, but Mike is essentially an informal speaker and is relaxed about waiting for the slides to catch him up.

The core presentational skill is putting together the right material in the right way. You need to discipline the story, get it concise. You have to tell it with the sort of clarity that you can all too easily avoid in day-to-day discussion.

Mike seems to present almost constantly, both internally and externally.

66 **The presentation is a trigger which helps you crystallize the strategy.** 99

66 **It forces you to constantly review what you have said before, so it acts as a sort of tracking mechanism; it keeps you focused on the strategy and keeps it alive.** 99

66 **In this sense our formal communications to some extent drive the process of strategic review. It is part of the strategic process.** 99

I once saw him give the same presentation seven times over a short period to small groups of senior managers at a business school. His enthusiasm for telling the story of Energis was as boundless at the end of the process as it had been at the beginning.

66 **Where you are giving the same presentation many times it is important not to let yourself get bored. Interacting with your audience is the best way to achieve this.** 99

The ability to take every audience seriously, and start communicating afresh however many times you have been over that same ground yourself, is an invaluable management skill.

Unusually for a man in his position with such a public role, Mike has a stammer. He prepares assiduously for presentations and often it is barely noticeable. He doesn't see it as an impediment at all, and to most Energis-watchers it is merely an occasional idiosyncrasy. But it does show that with sufficient determination, nothing need stand in your way.

66 **When you're standing at the lectern you are giving a performance. It's a bit like acting. You are very hyped up. Things like tempo and rhythm start to mean something.** 99

66 **Visibility is critical for a CEO and often being there, talking to your audience and provoking and answering their questions, is much more important than the content of the presentation. I think we need to move back from our obsession with content and look at the more human aspects of business.** 99

Energis regularly needs to give demonstrations of leading-edge technology and he is well used to the pitfalls.

> 66 **In my experience there is a 50 per cent chance of anything live in a presentation going wrong. I don't think this is necessarily a bad thing!** 99

> 66 **This can extend to the speakers themselves. In the middle of a joint presentation with Deutsche Telekom, one of their senior managers suddenly collapsed. For a moment I thought he was dead. Happily as it turned out he was just utterly exhausted after days without any proper sleep, and quickly recovered. But it does show the absurd pressure we allow corporate life to put us under. It could happen to any of us.** 99

Mike's presentations are technically straightforward – a great many bullet points interspersed with beautifully drawn maps. The overall style appears to owe little to PowerPoint due to the quality of the design and the art direction, but he and his team move so fast that they have to be able to put together a class presentation very quickly.

> 66 **Presentations are a core management skill. But they are also a team activity and it is really exciting when it all comes together really well and there's a buzz in the air and that last-minute rush of adrenalin as you get ready to start.** 99

Just like acting, after all.

Lucy Parker

Lucy has more influence on more senior presentations than anyone I know.

She's a coach. In much the same way as Turner was 'a painter'.

She is undoubtedly the leading practitioner in her field, and probably the most thoughtful. Her background is in the theatre and she began coaching business people almost by accident. She understands presentation and stagecraft, and fear and performance. And how these can be used creatively.

But these are secondary to the key issues.

Her constant themes are focus, coherency and ownership. Key to this is the process of simplification.

> 66 **Taking the core argument and reducing to something very simple, very easily communicated, very easy to hold in the mind and talk about. This is not a trivial exercise – you need to focus, to be disciplined, to challenge yourself.** 99

It is much more than just playing with words. It must be part of creating the thing itself – the expression of the central idea is part of bringing it into being. It will have a significant impact on what happens next.

Lucy adds:

> 66 **But more than that, it forces you to internalise and 'own' the central idea; it becomes something you are prepared to stand by; it is preparation for action.** 99

The central idea is then valid in every context. It does not have to be modified from audience to audience. It needs no 'spin'.

It takes great courage to do it properly. It is nothing to do with smooth talking. It is about sticking your head above the parapet. You are in the spotlight. On the record. So it is nerve-racking to many people. It is not the same as stage fright, but up there at the lectern it is easy to become suddenly self-conscious: suddenly what you are doing is significant.

That's scary.

> 66 **Many people don't pursue this process. They retreat into facts. More facts, they all too often believe, means a weightier argument. That's simply not true.** 99

Visual support can be very powerful, but no one should ever abdicate their argument to the slides. Often the critical message is not on the slide. Either because it shouldn't be there because it is the property of the speaker and he wants complete control of it (= good). Or because the critical issue, the telling judgement, has been ducked (= bad).

Visual support can be very powerful, but no one should ever abdicate their argument to the slides.

Speakers need to own what they say, and own the content of the slides.

 Our single biggest contribution is to help people define what they really want to communicate.

Lucy extends these concepts to the problems regularly faced by managers .

 Presenting upwards through the hierarchy can be intimidating for many people. It appears to be against natural authority. People need to understand that they are there because they know something their audience doesn't. This is their authority to present.

Faced with, say, a research report or a financial analysis, it is obviously proper to marshal all the facts.

 But the presentation lives elsewhere. You have a particular understanding of the facts and it is this understanding and interpretation that is the basis of the presentation, not the facts. This is very difficult for inexperienced presenters to grasp but is fundamental. Go beyond raw facts, get to the interpretation. It's what you *think* that matters.

Think too why you have been asked to present. What is the audience's relationship with these facts? Do they know them? Are they familiar with the format? Why do they want you to interpret them? Think about the people in the audience and how they relate to each other, and you to them.

 Use the presentation as a conversation, not a lecture.

Tell the story. This means having a start, a middle and an end, and knowing how you plan to journey between them. It does *not* mean spinning a yarn or putting a good spin on it.

Lucy at work is a real performer – a fascinating mixture of shrewd strategic vision, sheer hard work, unremitting concentration, and bullying effortlessly disguised as charming encouragement. And patience. In spades.

Howard Coates

Howard advises companies on how to manage their relations with investors, particularly institutional investors. He is concerned with the way the company presents its case, the way it is received by the institutions, and the way the company responds to comments or criticisms. As institutional power becomes concentrated into fewer and fewer hands, those that remain are better resourced and have become good and experienced industry watchers.

Research and knowledge are what gives an individual institution competitive advantage over its peers, so they work very hard at it.

> **Companies are increasingly conscious of competing for the investment dollar. They want to be investor-friendly, and this means explaining more about their business. As a result they have become much more professional at communicating, covering off all the bases that the institutional investor might want.**

So now all companies have to present well at a senior level. Having a poor presenter on his team is now a major problem for any CEO.

> **Many a share price has fallen after a bad presentation. Even in Europe companies are having to learn to present.**

It's a major discipline on management and a huge driver to get things done. In particular it forces them to crystallize strategies.

> **Strategy can be reviewed to your heart's content, but standing up and presenting it to a group of analysts or investors is something else entirely.**

Having a poor presenter on his team is now a major problem for any CEO.

66 **Some CEOs worry about every detail, others not at all. It tends to be driven less by industry sector than by the character of the CEO.** 99

Analysts value the Q&A session. They really do want to see senior management acting as a team – it's hugely important. So trust between the individuals in the team is critical and it quickly shows if it isn't there.

One analyst is noted for questioning management in a tone that implies that they are rather too dim to understand his question properly.

66 **A management that reacts negatively or defensively to this sort of thing sets the tone for the remainder of the meeting. You do need to manage the tone of the Q&A – hit a few sixes and get people on your side.** 99

Most companies make three to four announcements each year (interims, finals, annual general meeting, trading statements) which in turn dictate much of the management agenda. In addition, in recent years many companies have started to lay on an educational seminar where they can show the strength and depth of their second-tier management to analysts and investors. This gives them invaluable City exposure and vice versa.

Roles are changing. The company chairman is becoming less relevant, although some feel that they must get involved. Often they are disinclined to rehearse, and while this may suit their busy schedule it often puts the rest of the team at a disadvantage.

Mergers, acquisitions and hostile bids tend to be seen as a critical test of management. But apart from an abbreviated timescale and the frequent need to present under extreme pressure, the same considerations apply:

66 **It is essential to look closely at the issues surrounding the transaction. Investors' perceptions of these issues are very important and must be managed carefully.** 99

Technologies such as webcasting are becoming increasingly important.

❝ Webcasting has become a vital part of the corporate communication process. US regulation means companies must ensure a level playing field as far as investors are concerned and it's an important tool. The same is true in the UK. Webcasting is rapidly becoming routine. ❞

Tony Carlisle

Tony is a legend in financial PR. He commands enormous respect in the boardrooms of Britain. He is a Director of Incepta Group, one of the hot media stocks, and of Citigate Dewe Rogerson, its public relations arm.

He makes a case for pragmatism.

❝ In an ideal world you'd communicate one to one; but there isn't the time and doing so risks varying the message. Besides which, presentations are very cost effective. ❞

He splits the essence of financial presentations into three:

- the things you *want* to say;
- the things you *need* to say;
- the things you are *required* to say.

Few people, he believes, like doing presentations (although we feel this is less true in America where that presentational urge, just as some of us sometimes feel we need a good curry, is much stronger). Done well they take a long time to prepare, but the process of preparation crystallizes issues and often highlights flaws in arguments.

Technology has helped because nowadays things are more flexible and you can change things at the last moment. And while videoconferences make many feel uncomfortable Tony is convinced they will be the norm in ten years' time.

The holographic presentation is on its way too, he believes. So finally you will be able to present in two places at once. In person.

Audience expectations are shifting fast. Standards are rising. Brevity is the soul of the 21st century. We're entering an era of sound nibbles and sight bites. But behind them you have to have well argued substance.

Brevity is the soul of the 21st century. We're entering an era of sound nibbles and sight bites.

Years ago there were fewer but more razzmatazz presentations. The flotations were larger, more unusual (do you remember the excitement around the privatization of British Gas?). Now it's: 'Tell me the story. Get to the point.'

Today presentations need to add value and help management put over their message.

> **Presentations are conversations, not lectures; they represent business between consenting adults in public.**

Presentational style, argues Tony, should reflect the company's brand. He cites Orange as an example.

> **One of the great brands created in the nineties. Built on conviction, not confection, and their presentations have this in spades.**

Business is getting better at communicating, and more sophisticated too. Most businesses are adept at communicating a story of:

● a thoughtful strategy

● effectively executed

● with clear messages of where and how everything is going.

Most of all, arguments are getting clearer, simpler and stronger.

How do you judge a good presentation? It's like the proof of the pudding lying in the eating.

> **If it works.**

Q&As are critical. They show whether an individual really knows his job. They demonstrate the ability to persuade the audience.

In Europe, presentations have only recently become commonplace and are generally more prolix. Anglo-Saxon is generally more succinct culturally. Intriguingly:

> **First-rate marketing companies which deeply understand that the customer is king, still forget the audience is the customer of the day.**

Tony concludes with a warning and a piece of serious advice.

> **Never ever give a presentation unless it matters.**

Alan Parker

Alan is founder and Chairman of Brunswick Group, the most successful financial public relations business in Europe. (He was reputed to be worth £120 million (*Sunday Times*, 22 April 2001), so you should read this very, very carefully.)

> **Presentations are now a required part of business life. Anybody in any position of responsibility has to do them. Most people believe it is some sort of ritual where they have to play a part different from their normal self, so it can seem an alien form of communication to some.**

Many people seem to copy the style from elsewhere and go into mimic mode. They don't rely often enough on their own character, personality and style.

> **So you end up pretending to be what you're not – like a comedian going on a stage – as opposed to getting the audience involved with your thoughts and ideas.**

Alan is a fierce proponent of substance rather than style and believes there is too much stage craft nowadays. On the other hand, standards are rising, with more people being more competent. Fifteen years ago, there were no analyst or investor presentations. These were done by a marketing department whose need was to present everything so it looked better than it really was. (Those were the days when cynics called PR people and marketeers 'professional liars'.)

Alan feels live presentations are by far the most powerful. Technology will move people onscreen and online, but this will not displace live presentations, just as the annual report hasn't been eclipsed by analyst meetings.

> **Almost without exception the best performing companies in the world have the best communications systems in place.**

Communication is one of the fundamental jobs of management.

Communication is one of the fundamental jobs of management. It is the arterial system of the company without which nothing else functions.

The Listing Agreement with the Stock Exchange is an agreement that the chief executive will report on the progress of the business on a regular basis. This is 'a necessary good' and has helped improve standards of presentation overall. But it has to be questioned whether the amount of time that CEOs spend on investor relations is entirely productive.

> **Presentations are just one part of communications, but investor and media operations now take up to a third of a chief executive's time – and this excludes internal and customer relations.**

Alan sees presentations as part of an essential dialogue.

> **Presentations are not a one-way process. You have a platform to make your case when you present, but it must bring people together.**

He counsels against corporate theatre, against aggravating an audience, against letting the audience take control.

Managing expectation is critical, as is realizing not everything you plan to do will be universally popular.

> **Again, if you're making a case that is difficult for your audience to agree with, you must make it a two-way process.**
>
> **Sir Michael Edwardes at Dunlop was first class at this two-way communication. Most speakers don't prepare for their audience – they are too busy thinking about the points they want to make.**

Intriguingly it's often after the presentation itself – at the Q&A – that people start talking like real people.

Alan is suspicious of being dazzled by a great performance. Someone usually has to pick up the pieces afterwards. But for many there is a real fear of failure. There's a view that presentations are 'unreal'.

> **Presentations should be enjoyable for both presenter and audience and a "rightful nervousness" is a good and appropriate thing.**
>
> **But I'm nervous of speakers who are too smooth. There is a danger of confusing articulateness with brains.**

The best example of building a company by the power of its presentations, he agrees, was Hans Snook at Orange.

> **He used video extensively in what was essentially a marketing exercise.**

One of the most interesting recent developments, he feels, was Jeff Randall's move to the BBC in March 2001 to head up business reporting, a move which represents a sea change in the way business will be seen and appreciated by the public.

> **His move is very forward looking and represents an opportunity for programming for retail investors. It could lead to a whole different way of reporting.**

Alan is himself a much admired presenter, and his advice to others is simple:

> **Work out your story, what you want to communicate, before starting to write the presentation.**

And:

- dress in your own clothes;
- talk in your own voice;
- don't pretend to be someone else.

Finding a memorable way of saying it, well that's something else. He cites a Clinton sound bite:

> **There's nothing wrong with America that the right bits can't put right.**

66The audience got angry, then hostile ... he was lucky to escape unscathed.99

The best? No hesitation. Charles Handy to 120 people at ICL.

66It had the feel of a fireside chat – a quite intimate conversation – yet he did all the talking.99

Marcus reflects on change in presentations and draws a simple diagram.

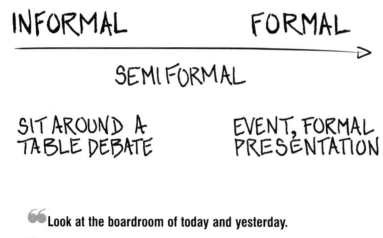

66Look at the boardroom of today and yesterday.

Yesterday the boardroom table, like the cabinet table, was designed for a debate. Today *everyone* designs their boardroom so presentations can be quickly and well set up.

I think presentations in the middle ground – reasonably small (say up to 50 people) – have gained share from either end.99

But in the final analysis, if you're really clear and skilled and a complete master at presenting, just one slide can do it for the audience. Marcus cites a colleague at Boston Consulting Group who presented a complex industry structure and strategy from one slide.

But as someone who is the son of one of the most stalwart of British actors – Terence Alexander – Marcus is focused on tone of voice.

Should you be humorous (and no, that doesn't mean telling a string of risqué jokes) or questioning? Fireside chat or MBA pointed questions? He describes a session he did with Andersen Consulting. Among the feedback questionnaires one read:

66 **This is clearly a man who is enjoying himself.** 99

There's a fair chance that if
you enjoy yourself, others will too.

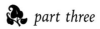 *part three*

PROPS, AIDS AND ZIMMER FRAMES –

The stuff that makes presentations work or fail

* *chapter nine*
  The use and abuse of visual aids   149

* *chapter ten*
  Sliding with confidence   156

* *chapter eleven*
  Fear of flying   169

* *chapter twelve*
  Getting it right on the night   180

* *chapter thirteen*
  Snatching triumph from the jaws of disaster   193

* *chapter fourteen*
  Taming the technicians   211

* *chapter fifteen*
  Presenting into the future   215

* **INSPIRERS, PERSPIRERS, ASPIRERS**   223
  Interviews with master presenters

Colin Prescot	– *Flying Pictures*
Paul Barratt	– *Gaskell*
Chris Milburn	– *Centrica*
2 senior civil servants	– *anonymous*
Jill Knight	– *Baroness and politician*
Kaizo Management Team	
Simon Walker	– *Communications Secretary for HM the Queen*

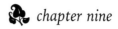

chapter nine

THE USE AND ABUSE OF

VISUAL AIDS

Visual aids and why they matter

Presenting is about having something to say. After-dinner speeches, wedding and bar mitzvah eulogies are often about having nothing to say and saying it beautifully, but presentations demand content.

Purely verbal content of any complexity is hard for an audience to take on board. In this television age audiences are no longer used to an unadulterated torrent of words. They need visual clues, signposts, stepping stones, visual punctuation. Visual aids are there to provide this.

Presentations generally consist of a presenter there, live and dangerous, and visual aids. These are usually shown on a screen or maybe a flipchart, or even (mainly in the US) printed out in 'decks' and placed in front of each member of the audience.

You and your visual aids have the floor. So what are the visual aids for? Why bother?

For the audience, visual aids are properly there for three reasons:

- to help them follow your line of argument
- to identify and highlight key points
- to help you illustrate and explain any subtle or complex points so that the audience can understand them more easily.

(And, sometimes legitimately, to remind speakers where they've got to.)

But visual aids are often used for many other reasons. To hide behind, to divert attention, to batter your way through a confused argument; too often they are used as a crutch, or are rushed and thoughtless, just stepping stones for the speaker.

Bad visual aids make
you look confused and inept.

They make you appear to have a less-than-full grasp of your subject. Over-busy visuals suggest to your audience that you cannot see the wood for the trees.

Really bad visuals – the ones where the writing is so small the audience can't read it, or which are designed so poorly they don't want to – suggest you are simply muddled or incompetent.

You see slides like these every day.

Would you wear an Oxfam suit for a major presentation to an important audience? Or a tie from Cheap'n'Easy? Yet people are doing the equivalent of dressing from the barrow in the local market for the day they're going to make the big impression: second-rate visual aids communicating a second-rate impression.

But like the emperor's new clothes, they see only what they want to see. They've got the words they want, the pictures they want, and all in the right order. So all is for the best in the best of all possible worlds.

And in a sense this is right. If you believe your visual aids are good enough for you, then they are. Belief is important. No one can present well with visual aids they hate.

But are they good enough for your audience?

Bad visuals don't mean that the presentation will necessarily be bad. But it does mean that from your first slide you are fighting an uphill battle to win your audience round.

As Edward Tufte says in his brilliant book *The Visual Display of Quantitative Information*:

'Clear graphics conveys clear thinking.'

Some people are great presenters despite their visual aids. Even with no visual aids at all. Some have great visuals, and a great speech, but still produce a boring, lifeless result.

So clearly visual aids alone cannot make a good presentation great. But done well, they help the audience and the speaker stay on song. And as the song says, 'that's what it's all about'.

The presentation cash register

If you really want to work out how long to talk for, find out the hourly rate of everyone in the room and add up the cost of ten minutes' talking. If you can get your message across in 15 minutes, can you justify the cost of the next ten?

Making great presentations

The more detailed the content of your presentation, the more important your visuals are. Not because every point needs its own slide – it doesn't – but because they help the audience understand your key points and remember them.

So, just hand a list of headlines and bullet points to your secretary and the job's done.

No. No. No.

There are plenty of secretaries who do great visual aids. Those who have the time, the inclination and the know-how, and a certain flair for graphics. And the sense to keep things simple despite the blandishments of their boss.

Good visual aids are invisible; they become **part of the experience.**

Creating good slides depends on properly understanding what it is you are trying to communicate and how unnecessary clutter can be stripped away. This must be done not just in the context of a single slide but also of the presentation as a whole. Which is why slides added as an afterthought often do not 'belong' – the rest of the presentation simply did not take them into account.

Presenting with your secretary

Secretaries will never learn to understand the dynamics of presentations because they never get to see them. The only way for them to understand what works and what doesn't and so contribute positively is for them to become a partner in the process. Get your secretary into the presentations (not just the rehearsal) to watch you, to comment, to criticize. And even stand at the lectern and present it for you to judge.

Teamwork, as always, pays dividends.

There is no 'best' way to create a slide; you do what works for you. But look hard at each slide to see whether it really does help your audience understand the point you are making. If it doesn't, drop it or change it. Think too how you might do it better, more simply, more visually, more graphically.

There are **no rules** that **can't be broken** by experienced presenters who know what they are doing.

I have seen Terry Leahy, CEO of Tesco, give a presentation where he looked at each slide, read it out to the audience as if slightly surprised to find it there, then spoke effortlessly without notes on that particular aspect of the business.

'Slide as agenda' if you like.

His technique extended to talking to individuals in the audience by name, and drawing on their experience in support of the points he was making. There was nothing gratuitous in this. He had everyone's attention from beginning to end. In part this was because he might suddenly turn to *you*, but it was mainly due to his skill in weaving the threads of individual stories into a relevant and dynamic whole.

I saw Jonathan Wootliff, formerly of Greenpeace, use about 100 text slides in a 15-minute presentation. Sounds ghastly. But each had a single word, perhaps two at most. The impact was electrifying – fast-paced, confident, sweeping the audience along with him as he went.

Christopher Davis of Dorling Kindersley had my vote for potentially the worst presentation ever at an international conference – 141 slides, all pictures, in a ten-minute presentation. That works out at four seconds a slide.

I thought he **was mad.**

Instead it was a *tour de force*, making one single point about his company's philosophy and products brilliantly and apparently without effort. Every picture was there for a reason and the dialogue was precisely calculated to work with each picture.

An effortless performance, achieved only with a lot of hard work.

There is a view that the Cold War was ended with a presentation that comprised just two pictures. Knowing President Reagan's distaste for long, tightly argued documents, he was shown first a picture of a scruffy, ill-equipped apology for a soldier, followed by one of a smartly turned-out, superbly equipped marine.

Then all it took was a simple question: 'Which do you want our boys to look like?' and the money flowed and the Russians were priced out of the game.

Sometimes a presentation doesn't need to argue; it just needs to push at an open door.

chapter ten

SLIDING WITH CONFIDENCE

Making slides work for you

There are really only three main types of slide. The text slide, the graphic slide and the blank slide.

The text slide

The text slide – words, words, words, perhaps with bullets and even (if you must) sub-bullets (not, please God, sub-sub-bullets, the sure sign of a cad and a bounder).

Text slides are the great stand-by. Anyone can (and does) do them. To death. There is nothing whatsoever wrong with them except that if you use them badly they can quickly make a presentation look and feel utterly boring. We've all had to sit through slide after slide of headline and bullet points and wished we were somewhere else. Anywhere else.

But we are the PowerPoint generation and this is what we do. Death by bullet point is the undeserved fate of many an audience in the hands of a poor presenter.

Many corporate templates give you instructions like 'not more than five bullets', 'not more than ten words per bullet', and they are undoubtedly all absolutely right. But however good such prescriptive advice, experienced presenters will make their own judgements, and often find ways to avoid using them altogether.

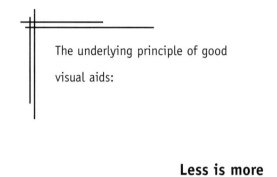

The underlying principle of good visual aids:

Less is more

It's obvious really.

The more words you put on a slide, the less impact they have.

And the less hard the slide works for you. Wordy slides have other disadvantages. They are harder to read. They require conscious effort on the part of the audience, and while they are reading and puzzling out your meaning they are not listening to you.

While they're reading your slide they're **not listening to you.**

A short slide is much more flexible than a long one. A slide full of details about your distribution arrangements will need changing with every variation of the plan. A slide that simply highlights the key issues may need changing much less often.

Long, wordy slides may feel safe, but they are a snare and a delusion; they lock you in very specific lines of argument. Short slides of key issues give you endless flexibility to re-interpret them, work them, and respond to your particular audience's interests and expectations.

Short slides of key issues give you endless flexibility.

And when you make a presentation where your slides need to be signed off by your lawyers, you will appreciate anew the advantages in cost and time of short, simple slides.

While the time needed to make alterations may not be a major issue in a short presentation, in longer ones the amount of time required for last-minute changes can be a serious problem, especially when handouts have to be printed. A speaker wanting 'half an hour of changes' always needs a good hour by the time he has briefed the changes, the work has been done, and he has checked it. So eight speakers at a conference each wanting just a few changes can easily add a whole extra day, and disrupt the best laid plans.

But sometimes, word slides full of detail are unavoidable. So how best to use them?

There are three different sorts of word slide which can be characterized as 'top down', 'bottom up' or 'flat'.

The 'top down' or exposition slide starts with a proposition in the headline and then has a number of text points to amplify it, to move the argument forward. After the speaker has finished with the slide we have all moved on with him. These slides, properly used, are dynamic and help a presentation to flow.

Fig. 10.1 A 'top-down' or exposition slide.

Northern Region Success

- Sales on budget
- Margins up
- Distribution gains

Now #1 brand

The 'bottom up' or justification slide starts with a proposition and seeks to justify it. At the end of the slide we are pretty much where we were at the beginning, but hopefully with rather more understanding.

Fig. 10.2 A 'bottom-up' or justification slide.

Sales up 10%

UK	:	+5%
Europe	:	+5%
US	:	+15%
MEA	:	−10%
RoW	:	−5%

They are useful where detailed points need close examination, but they should be used with care as they can make presentations lurch forward from one slide to the next. Sales charts are common examples.

This way of presenting – exposition and justification – is deeply embedded into the PowerPoint view of the world. It is perfectly acceptable as far as it goes. But it can become boring if used excessively.

The 'flat' slide is pretty much anything else. A single word, a phrase, a statement, a quotation. Whatever.

Once you have got out of the bullet point phase, flat slides are the workhorse of a presentation. They are neutral; they let you move an audience in any direction; and the way the presentation flows is dictated entirely by the speaker.

The graphic slide

Pictures, charts or drawings where any text is subsidiary. A picture, in the time-honoured phrase, is worth ten thousand words.

Words themselves can be graphic objects if they are few enough, big enough and dramatic enough. The test is whether they can be assimilated by the audience without overtly being read.

Graphics slides, properly designed, can be much more effective than a wordy description – simple to absorb, interesting to look at, quick to impart significant information, carefully stripped of anything unnecessary or distracting. They should be distinctive and memorable. When they are, they enliven a presentation and give it style and panache.

Complex ideas are usually best presented in a series of simple steps, each building up the overall picture.

It can be very much quicker to take an audience through a ten-stage build of, say, the workings of an industrial process than to show the whole thing in a single slide and try to explain it. This same principle is just as true for number charts, research results or a lecture on the human skeleton. Start simple. Move on in simple steps.

The blank slide

Much neglected. It does not need to be entirely blank, of course. It might have the title of the presentation or the logo or name of the event.

It is what you put on the screen when you don't want anything on the screen.

> But a completely empty screen can just look like a mistake and so distract the audience.

In developing a presentation you should be conscious not only of what slide you want to appear and when, but also when you want it to disappear. Don't make the mistake of leaving an inappropriate slide on the screen when the subject matter has moved on; this confuses the audience and detracts from your argument.

Some very effective presenters use blanks almost entirely, which gives disproportionate emphasis to the slides they do use.

A variation on this is to put up a simple but enigmatic slide at the start of the presentation, then ignore it until you are about to leave the stage (to the growing alarm of the audience). At the last moment you glance up at it and say, 'Oh, yes ...' It is the presentational equivalent of pulling rabbits out of hats and there is a fine description of Tom Peters doing just that in Chapter One.

Fine if you are Tom Peters, but choose your moment.

The running, jumping, standing-still show

Builds, animation and transitions can all provide movement and excitement to your slides. In moderation. But too much will quickly irritate your audience. Instead of showing a lightness of touch, it becomes too clever, too slow, too overt, and starts to intrude between the speaker and the audience.

In general, builds should match text development, and transitions should be used only where relevant – for example a line graph that 'wipes on' from left to right is a natural and relevant way of emphasizing that it is a time series.

Quality animations are starting to become possible in PowerPoint, but judge whether these are meaningful or merely self-indulgent and distracting to the audience.

At a recent conference a presentation started with a wonderful animated sequence of moving squares that resolved itself, after several minutes, into the title. Brilliant programming, a real tour de force. But it left the audience cold. They were there for business, not gameshows.

PowerPoint is filled with effects, mostly for beginners. Just because you can do it doesn't mean you should do it.

Remember that the hero of the presentation is you, the speaker, never the visual aids. Good visual aids can make you look confident, feel great and demonstrate clear thinking and grasp of your subject. But nobody has come to see them – they've come to see you and hear you.

You want them to go out saying, 'Great presentation – let's do it.'

Only designers go out saying, 'Great visuals.'

In the very early days when we used Apple IIs and electronic presentations were virtually unheard of, a client's presentation to a potential German customer was stopped mid-way through when he leapt up. 'What you are showing me on this screen is not possible,' he cried. 'Computers can't do this. What's going on?'

This was a failure. We had let the technology get in the way of the argument.

But it had a happy ending. He bought the deal. And one of our presentation systems.

Consistency and inconsistency

Consistency of visual style is important. It helps define your voice, it makes you look coherent and is therefore reassuring to your audience. Once they have got the hang of your style – after perhaps two or three slides – they can assimilate further material quickly and without alarm.

Consistency shouldn't mean boring. It mostly means attention to obvious details such as keeping fonts and type sizes in line; keeping headlines in the same place so they don't appear to jump around as you move from slide to slide; keeping colours under control.

In this context the deliberately different slide can then have considerable impact.

The tyranny of the design template

Some organizations insist on a corporate 'look', with design templates and strict rules about what you can and can't do, often for very good reasons which they can no doubt explain to you.

This 'lowest common denominator' style of working is designed to achieve a minimum standard for all presentations and ensure that material from one presentation can be re-used in another. Both commendable objectives.

In practice they are often full of traps for the unwary. The most common is finding a logo in the bottom right-hand corner of the slide, just where the 'total' figure on financial slides needs to go; or in the top right or left where it interferes with every headline you ever want to write.

the practised presenter
will easily subvert

The practised presenter will easily subvert (without altogether abandoning) the corporate style and allow his or her own voice to come through.

Pace and timing

(Or which comes first: the script or the slides?)

Presentations can be constructed either script first, slides second, or the other way round. In both cases drafting one, then the other, revising one, revising the other, and so on, can lead to a satisfactory presentation.

But the advantage of drafting the visuals first is that in blocking out the main points as charts, a rhythm is established that generally carries through to the finished product. There is nothing exact about this rhythm, but the pattern, the sense of regular progression, quickly becomes apparent.

It is harder to establish such a rhythm in presentations that start as scripts, and the result can easily be a flurry of charts followed by long gaps. Or several bullet points appearing in quick succession, then several minutes before the next.

This feels odd and disjointed. It is disconcerting for the audience and undermines their concentration on the speaker. Waiting for the other shoe to drop.

If you have to prepare a presentation from a script, bear these difficulties in mind. But given the choice, always start with the visuals and develop the speech from them.

Short and sweet

As we have seen, by and large the fewer words on a slide, the more impact the slide has. The slide that says everything says nothing.

The slide that says everything
says nothing.

But beware of unintended meanings. As you shorten text, you will have a particular interpretation in your head, but others may see it differently.

An example of this occurred (so the story has it) when the first stick deodorant was launched in Britain. Deodorants were new, the concept of a stick deodorant was new, and so the instructions were carefully worded: 'Remove the top from the tube, push the base up until the deodorant stick protrudes about half an inch, and rub it gently on the skin.' However, research showed that the logo had to be bigger and so the copy had to be cut down a little. And the ingredients had to be listed and the copy had to be cut a little more. Then the weight had to be added, and the copy cut again, and so on.

At the launch party thrown by the advertising agency to celebrate this wonderful new product, the champagne flowed and everyone was in high spirits. But a young executive who didn't know anyone very much and felt a bit left out of it all idly picked up a pack and started to examine it. He read the instructions. Horrified, he went to the advertising director and said, 'We can't launch this. Look.' The advertising director in turn went to the marketing director, and the whole thing was pulled.

The reason? The instructions for use, pared to the bone, now said simply: 'Remove top and push up bottom.'

Remove top and push up bottom.

A classic example of knowing so clearly what you mean that you forget what it is you say.

Similar problems of unintentional or dual meanings often occur with bullet points or abbreviated sentences such as headlines. Like the famous headline from the war:

French push
bottles up Germans

A small change in the layout has a remarkable effect:

French push bottles
up Germans

Or Flanders & Swann's wonderful double switch in expectation in their song *Ill Wind* (sung exuberantly to the tune of Mozart's *Fourth Horn Concerto*):

I lost my horn ...

I lost my horn ...

I *found* my horn ...

... gawn

Help your audience stay on side. Make things easy for them.

Make sure you make sense.

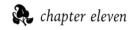

chapter eleven

FEAR OF FLYING

Honing the cutting edge

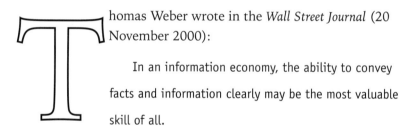homas Weber wrote in the *Wall Street Journal* (20 November 2000):

> In an information economy, the ability to convey facts and information clearly may be the most valuable skill of all.

What's the easiest way to improve the clarity of your next presentation?

Here are three steps. See how brave you are.

1. *Take out all the sub-bullet points.*
   That's pretty easy, almost painless – a few cherished references, perhaps, but they're in the speech anyway.

2. *Remove everything else you can.*
   Go through every headline and every bullet taking out every unnecessary word, every relative clause, every inessential

verb or adjective, even every bullet that doesn't make a big difference.

Now you are starting to make big points – the speech can take care of the context and the subtleties.

3. *Take out all the bullet points* (much harder this).
Every single one. Even all the ones you have just cut down. Then drop all the headlines down into the middle of the page and double the point size. An adjustment here, a refinement there, and you've kicked away the crutches – you have a real presentation. And audiences everywhere will love you.

> you've kicked away the crutches – you have a **real presentation**

'Ah!' I hear you say, 'They need to have all this information I've just cut out.' No problem – put it in the handout. But do they really need it to understand your big point? Or do you?

Highlighting and lowlighting

Now you have cut the fat from your presentation, you will want to make the core material work harder. Here the technique of dynamically highlighting (and its converse – lowlighting) can be very useful. The effects must match your speech.

Highlighting can be done by changing the colour of text, by placing a contrasting box behind the text, by enlarging the text, by isolating the text on the page or by combining some or all of these things.

By contrast, lowlighting removes emphasis and shows you have moved on. It is often done by changing the colour of text to grey or a tone of the background colour. When combined with a 'build' slide the effect can be dynamic and imparts a strong sense of forward movement.

On busy or complex charts these techniques can be used to isolate and draw attention to specific information, and as the speaker moves on, so can the highlight.

Done properly, these techniques seem entirely natural from the audience's viewpoint – they see such things every night on the news.

Presenting by numbers

Presenting numbers is common in business but often viewed with trepidation by presenters and audiences alike. Yet numbers are relatively easy to present.

Every number tells a story and there are many different ways of presenting them. First, know your audience. Analysts, well versed in detailed numbers, are unlikely to want to see your P&L in graphical form, even if that will charm your elderly investors at the AGM.

> unlikely to want to see your P&L in graphical form

By all means include graphs of five-year trends, or deal with historic figures in an artistic way (unless they have been restated). But audiences who feed on numbers will be suspicious of new or unfamiliar numbers presented in anything other than their raw state.

Graphs and charts

Graphs and charts can hugely simplify the presentation of data. They can also obfuscate and confuse. Keep them simple. Label them clearly. Avoid distortion. Be wary of large numbers of data points labelled with countless small and illegible labels. And read Edward Tufte's *Envisioning Information* (he dislikes PowerPoint, by the way, regarding it as effectively reducing the sum of human knowledge).

In his book *Visual Explanations* Professor Tufte analyzes the space shuttle explosion in January 1986 caused by a flaw in the O-rings. The engineers had data showing the likely effect of low temperatures well before the launch but failed to persuade their managers of the problem. The data was presented ineptly (the engineers were not trained or experienced presenters, they were just rocket scientists) and the problem simply did not show up convincingly.

Professor Tufte uses simple graphs to illustrate how the case for postponement could have been made compelling.

Seven people died as millions watched, horrified, on television.

Good presentation
really does matter.

Financial graphs need to be handled scrupulously. You may be able to get away with a non-zero baseline if you explain carefully that you are deliberately exaggerating the differences in order to highlight them. But don't try to slip it through as it will undermine your credibility elsewhere.

If you are presenting research numbers to marketing people, the reverse is true. Here you are looking to highlight trends and patterns, and good graphics can reveal and convey these with a depth and richness of content that numbers alone can never do.

Remember that if you are familiar with the numbers or graphs but the audience is not, your quick summary will be lost on them. It will take them some time to assimilate a new chart; and unless they are already familiar with your style they simply won't be able to take in a pie chart with 17 segments, or the group of pies, or the seven-line graph.

If you have a series of similar charts, take immense care over the way you explain the first. Once the audience has got the hang of it, you can fire off as many more at them as you wish and they will understand each of them almost immediately.

The Cold Mother Test

Try the Cold Mother Test (if your own mother isn't available, any passing mother will do). Hand her a printout of the graph, cold (i.e. without any explanation) and ask her to tell you what it means. If it is obvious to her, then you're OK. If she has to fetch her glasses, you're already in trouble. If, even with her glasses she doesn't understand and can't immediately explain it, even your most supportive audience won't.

They really won't.

Simplify all graphs and all numbers down to the basic point you're trying to communicate. Put everything else – the full table, the complete data set with all the labels, whatever – in an appendix. Or drop it.

Design matters

Many presenters are content to take a standard PowerPoint template, black text on white, and simply hammer out their presentation. The result is perfectly adequate for many purposes, for internal meetings, briefing sessions and so on. But the value of design lies in what it says

- about you
- about what you think of your audience
- about what you think of your subject matter.

Under-design sends out all sorts of messages about lack of caring, preparation, thoughtfulness. Over-design is nearly as bad. Trying too hard may make the audience feel that they are looking at a pre-packaged solution, that content has been sacrificed to form.

Good design is not necessarily slower or more expensive **than any other sort of design.**

Nor do you need an expensive design consultancy to do it for you. It is simply a question of being appropriate for the task.

Design should of course take into account the style of the speaker, the type of audience, and the content of the presentation. But the environment also matters – not just the venue, lighting and staging, but the computer's capabilities too, and particularly its handling of fonts.

Design matters. Remember the row over the 'butterfly' design of some of the voting forms used in Florida during the 2000 presidential elections? Amazon.com, feted for its user-friendly web site, displayed a spoof version designed along the lines of such a ballot paper. To find the book of your choice you had to follow the correct arrow and 'punch' a hole, just as the voters were controversially required to do.

Design that was good enough for electing a new president would, they reckoned, have put them out of business in a matter of weeks.

Fonts

Many people would like to use something more interesting than everyday fonts like Arial and Times New Roman. But if you are going to distribute your presentation or run it on computers other than your own, you may run into all sorts of problems, from licensing agreements to embedding properties.

Get this wrong and your presentations will start to go haywire as fonts are automatically substituted and line-endings over-run, tables no longer align, and worse.

Great fonts give character and distinction to your presentations. But it is a complicated area for the unwary and you should get specialist advice if you have such ambitions.

Great fonts give character and distinction to your presentations.

Other visual aids (and non-visual aids)

There are many other sorts of visual aids besides those projected on to the screen. Charles Laughton, as the melodramatic lawyer who reveals the dagger – 'aah, the murder weapon' – to gasps of horror from the assembled court, is simply using a visual aid.

Lady Macbeth achieved much the same effect with an *invisible* visual aid, which should be a lesson to us all.

Real objects – the book, the toy, the gear-housing, whatever – can be used productively. Hold them up. Talk to them. Bang them. Break them. Stir them. Drop them.

> Hold them up. Talk to them. Bang them. Break them. Stir them. Drop them.

But use them.

And like Terry Leahy, the CEO of Tesco, use the audience as a visual aid. Talk of individuals by name, point them out and remind them of how they solved this sort of problem. Make them out to be heroes, repositories of important and useful experience and information. Personalize. It can be a very effective technique in internal presentations as it brings (or appears to bring) people on-side and so predisposes others to follow.

It also concentrates the minds of everyone present in case they're the one who might be singled out next.

Jokes

Jokes are another aid, usually non-visual. Avoid them.

If you are really comfortable with them and know how to make an audience laugh, you will instinctively know just when and where to break this rule. But nothing is worse than a joke that falls flat. So if you are in any doubt, avoid it.

Jokes are a problem for most presenters (particularly to a new audience) because it is difficult to establish the *expectation* of humour. If you have a reputation for telling jokes you may be able to use it to advantage in an in-house gathering, but beware of the external audience. All great comedians can have an audience in stitches without ever doing anything or saying anything of significance, purely because of the sense of expectation. It is possible to build this from scratch, as the story of Jack Dee on page 68 shows; but remember, he had got to the 'sod 'em all' stage by then (which, hopefully, won't be your situation).

An audience may laugh at their CEO's jokes but this may not always have a great deal to do with their being funny.

Humour is different. Dry asides, irony, self-deprecation, wit – all make the presentation more interesting, more human, more memorable. You're not seeking outright laughter (although on a good day you may get it), but the audience will feel appreciated and if they feel good about themselves they'll feel good about you.

If you want a masterclass in comic delivery.

If you want a masterclass in comic delivery, study Gerard Hoffnung's recording of his 'Bricklayer' story which he told to the Oxford Union in the sixties. A simple story, simply told, of a bricklayer collecting excess bricks from a roof where he had been working, and slightly hurting himself in the process.

Not very promising material.

But timing, repetition, pauses and tone of voice, as well as the ability to nudge an audience along in the direction they were all happy to go, made for several minutes of pure delight out of almost thin air.

But beware: humour doesn't travel well and it doesn't translate. Not even between countries sharing a common language (perhaps particularly not there).

Handy hints on handouts

Handouts serve three main purposes – as a reminder of your presentation, as a place to take notes during the presentation, and as a digest of facts and figures.

In the mid-nineties the average handout was a black-and-white photocopy stapled in one corner. Most still are. But now they regularly form a sophisticated part of the corporate communications programme, with quality colour printing, extensive notes and appendices, and proper binding.

What works well for slides doesn't automatically work well on paper. Indeed some presentations need to be reworked extensively for print if the handouts are to be useful in their own right.

What works well for slides **doesn't automatically** work well on paper.

You can use a much smaller type size on paper than on projected slides, so charts that are best split in two or even three on screen can be brought back together in the handout. And you can add detail that is inappropriate on the screen – supporting arguments, additional figures and so on – as notes to the charts to provide depth and background information.

Appendices, inserts, pre-printed covers, even pre-printed paper, all help turn an inexpensive handout into a professional piece of communication.

Video

An extreme form of graphics is the video.

Video can be the hero of the hour, producing a real buzz of anticipation and excitement. It is also the quickest way to lose control of your audience as you break the magic thread of storytelling, the bond you have carefully built between you and them.

Used wisely (which usually means in very short bursts) it can hugely enhance a presentation, but many an event has been killed stone-dead by showing the corporate video as the high point of the day. Good or bad, it can be hard to recover the audience's attention and reassert your control.

Nevertheless, it is becoming much easier to incorporate video into the heart of your presentation. Techniques commonplace on television and therefore natural to audiences are becoming easier with digital formats and the new generation of 'video-windows' products.

How do you put all these things together? David Reed of Whitbread nicely summarizes the problem:

66The nature of presentations is changing. On the one hand there is demand for more disclosure and at the same time there is pressure for brevity.99

It can take **ten times as long to create a short presentation** as it does a longer one.

chapter twelve

GETTING IT RIGHT

ON THE NIGHT

Making it all work on stage

Remember the Labour and Conservative Party conferences in 1996?

The Conservative team arrived on the platform not knowing where they were to sit; worse, their names were shown marked on the front of the table so the audience could identify them, but nobody had thought to make them readable from behind, where the politicians were milling about. No one knew where to go. Chaos. It gave the impression of a disorganized bunch of well-meaning amateurs.

In contrast, Labour appeared in the right order – the same order as their seats – knew exactly where to sit, sat down, and got on with the conference. They looked more alert, more efficient, more professional. And they won the election.

Rehearsals

So rehearsal means a lot more than practising your lines. It means deciding how to get on and how to get off, where to sit, where to stand, and what to do before your presentation. And after it.

Rehearsals are important, especially when you are trying to coordinate with other speakers or need technicians to do complicated things with perfect timing.

Over-rehearsing is a sign of anxiety and will only make you stale. A degree of mild confusion can give an attractive sense of spontaneity. But don't overdo it.

> A degree of mild confusion can **give an attractive sense** of spontaneity.

Sometimes you will have to rehearse with paper printouts of your presentation. Helpful, but only up to a point. If your visuals are at all ambitious, the builds, transitions and animations will have a dynamic quality totally lacking on the paper version. You will rehearse the easy parts, and fail to rehearse the parts where you need to interact most closely with the visuals.

Rehearse with your spouse or children. Good family politics to keep them in the loop, and you will be astonished how much of a good presentation they understand – you undoubtedly use office jargon at home all the time without really thinking about it.

And that's the point. They should understand it. If they don't, who will? They are more on your side than any audience, they want you to make it work, they want you to tell them what drives or excites you. If you can't get it across to them – however technical the content – you won't get it across to many in your audience.

Try getting your secretary to present it to you. If you get bored half way, think what your audience will feel. It will give you a good idea of how well the slides are working with the speech. You'll learn; your secretary will learn.

Presentations are plastic – they can and should be bent and stretched and generally abused until they are in the shape you want. Get a good PowerPoint operator to work with you and together you can create magic.

There is one downside to rehearsals. If you are a supplier waiting, for example, for sign-off to print 350 handouts in colour, collate and bind them and deliver them to an early morning meeting, all too often you find that the client, flushed with success after his evening rehearsal, goes off to dinner and simply forgets. Leaving his prints – not to mention everybody else's evening – in tatters.

Working your slides

If you study how speakers 'work' their slides you will find three main schools. There are those who ignore their slides, regarding them as just a decorative aside, there to keep the slow ones in the audience on track but otherwise to be left in peace.

Then there are those who regard their slides as the presentation itself and admire them so much that they turn their backs (physically or metaphorically) on their audience and talk the slides through point by point.

And finally, there are those who regard the screen as a partner, an ally. They will draw the audience's attention to it when appropriate, but not be locked into it.

66 Look at this sales increase. 25 per cent.

How did we get there? Well ... 99

Builds, transitions and animations all draw the attention of the audience to the screen and therefore away from the presenter. You will have done this deliberately (won't you?), so work the screen – 'building on that point we find …' – don't let the screen work you. Anticipate the effect and use it.

Working acetates is very different from working computer slides. They are a much more personal, hands-on medium. By adding layers to a base acetate, by drawing on them and annotating them, you can bring the audience into the process and make the presentation an evolving, living experience. For all the low technology involved, you can give great presentations with acetates.

you can bring the audience into the process and make the presentation an evolving, living experience

But not with 'decks'. Although largely an American phenomenon, most I have seen should be buried without trace. Decks are humble handouts elevated to the status of star turn. They are emergency rations and should be treated as such. They reduce the presenter to compère and by dissipating the focus and energy of a presentation, negate most of what a skilled presenter can bring to bear.

Flipcharts, interactive multimedia presentations on laptops and so on can all perform for some people some of the time. A really good presenter can do wonders with just a paper bag and a felt tip pen, but back where most of us work it is PowerPoint or equivalent, up on a screen.

And very good it can be too.

Should you read out your slides?

A lot of blood has been spilt on this one. Even our interviewees had very different views.

We think it is easy to resolve.

Most charts, long or short, contain a number of key words, phrases or numbers. Maybe part of the headline, perhaps the first words in several bullet points, possibly a complete phrase. They pretty much define the point of the chart for your purposes.

Go through these key words at the outset and the audience will make sense of the chart very quickly, and understand why it is there.

But if you avoid using them they will be searching the chart for clues to the meaning and context and so not listening to you properly.

So the 'to read or not to read' problem can be restated: identify and use the key words. Having helped the audience grasp the point of the chart by the use of key words, do you then spell out the rest or do you get on with the presentation?

identify and use the
key words

Normally there is no advantage to be gained by reading out the non-essential stuff – the audience will be there way before you.

But you must use the right words early to make the link.

Some charts are written with few, if any, key words – a quotation, for example – and may well be sensibly read in full if only for emphasis. And some speakers write their charts in such a way that reading them in full is an innate part of what they do. Fine.

But making the connection to your chart is essential, whether it is full of detailed figures or contains just a simple graphic. So speak to your chart; use words that are on your chart; but reading every word is usually unnecessary.

Don't ignore your chart.
Presumably it's there for a reason.

Don't chart one thing and say another, especially with numbers. A common mistake in financial charts is to display percentage differences but speak about net differences – leaving the audience searching for the figure and quickly losing contact with the speaker. You are in effect asking them to do mental arithmetic while still following your argument.

	This Year	Last Year	Change
Sales	£277.6m	£248.9m	+12%

In this example you and I both know that when the speaker talks of £28.7m he is referring to the 12%. But in a chart containing several rows of numbers, this may not be obvious to everybody else. They will quickly get lost.

So make sure that your key words and numbers are on the slide; and be very wary of using numbers that are not on the slide.

Reading your script

Some presentations require you, for legal reasons, to read your script. Word for word. Most don't. So don't.

If you are going to use a script, find a good script writer. And when you've found them, hang on to them – like good wine, they only get better with age as they start to learn your interests and enthusiasms and can judge how to make your personality come to the fore.

At all costs avoid scripts written by lawyers and bankers. They like proper grammar, subordinate clauses, infinitives that don't split and all the other things that real people don't do when they speak.

Once you have a good script it will be all the better for acting as your guide and comforter and not taken too literally.

Learn to speak from notes so that you can dispense with a script; these you can carry in one hand as you pace about the stage or even into the audience.

This way you become your own best visual aid.

Once you have mastered notes, you can start to reduce them to a single card with a few cryptic comments. And then you are within reach of the presenter's nirvana – the scriptless, noteless, apparently improvized presentation.

But remember Mark Twain: 'I charge twice as much for an extemporaneous talk, because it takes me twice as long to prepare for it.'

In his book on speechmaking, *High Impact Business Presentations*, Lee Bowman describes a technique for reading from a script you have never seen before. It is effective with any script.

You look purposefully at your audience.

You look down at your script.

You commit a phrase to memory. No rush.

You look up.

You look at your audience.

You say the phrase.

You continue to look at your audience.

You look down for the next phrase.

And so on.

Described like this it sounds dreadful – slow, mannered, boring. But in practice it comes across as considered, thoughtful and weighty. It gives a strong impression of talking to the audience, not reading from a script. And once you get the hang of the technique it frees you from the lectern – you can come out of hiding and be with the audience, talk to them, not just speak to them.

It gives a **strong impression** of talking to the audience, not reading from a script.

And all from a script you have never seen before. Just think what you could do with a script you know!

The blank slide, the silent comment

Not every point needs a slide.

In fact, often the most telling points can be made without a slide at all.

Blank slides can fill in gaps when no slide is appropriate, but they can also signal a momentous message, a key pronouncement. They focus the audience's attention strongly on you, the speaker.

Equally, sometimes the most emphatic thing you can do in a presentation is shut up.

Not speak.

Stay silent.

The effect is electrifying.

Practise a five-second pause.

One hundred
(wait ...)

Two hundred

Three hundred

Four hundred

Five hundred

Good? Now try six, seven, ten seconds.

Dare you do more?

15?

20? (Oh my God, he's dried up)

Pauses, properly handled, make you look intelligent, thoughtful, considered, weighty.

Presenting is not like television.

You do not need to throw a constant stream of noise and pictures at your audience.

Autocues and other excitements

There are those who like autocues (teleprompters) and those who don't. If it works for you, fine. But aim to move on in due course. They trap you physically, rooting you to one particular spot. And they lock you into a very fixed speech.

Like all technology, autocues will sometimes go wrong or the operators will misjudge your expectations. So work on the principle that it will fail just when you need it most. Have a script with you; turn the pages as you speak so you can quickly transfer if you need to.

And avoid the experience of one speaker who felt the autocue was going a bit fast, so he spoke faster. As a result the operator speeded up, so the speech went faster still, and so on and on until an exhausted, breathless speaker finally had to capitulate.

The autocue operator's livelihood depends on their ability to react to unseen, unspoken messages from virtual strangers (you) and most are pretty good at it. The easiest way to slow down is simply that.

Slow down.

Or even stop.

Platform behaviour

How is your platform etiquette?

Jangling your change?

– take it out of your pockets and put it in your briefcase.

Turning your back on your audience?

– of course you don't.

Over-running your time slot?

– it is bad manners to your host and to your audience.

Hands in your pockets?

– surely not.

Turning away from your fixed microphone?

– so you don't want to be heard?

There are countless books written about such matters and most of the solutions are simple. The underlying principle is respect for your audience. If you have it, everything else flows naturally. Pretty much.

The semi-formal presentation is fast becoming the norm. The very informal and the very formal presentation still have their place, but increasingly you will find it appropriate and comfortable to step away from the lectern, or lean on it from the side, or relax on a high stool, and simply talk. Lecterns make a great focus on stage, but beware of the tendency to hide behind them.

beware of the tendency to hide behind them

In such a world it is OK to ask the operator for the next slide ('John, show me the next slide. No, the next. That's the one. OK') or to go back or forward. You can abandon your slides or flip through them fast if time is running out. Everything is OK as long as it is in the interests of the audience. And you feel comfortable doing it. But if you're uncomfortable the audience will quickly sense it and become uncomfortable too.

Just don't jangle the change in your pocket.

The striptease – how to hold your audience's attention

Have you ever tried taking your clothes off on stage? Men-only stuff this. Introduce yourself and start talking. Then take your jacket off. After a few minutes, roll up your sleeves, quite deliberately, one at a time. After a few minutes more, loosen your tie. As the presentation comes to an end, reverse the process, tighten your tie, button up your sleeves and as you conclude, put your jacket back on.

Why? The effect is curious. It makes your audience relax. It drags them into involvement with you. It is highly manipulative but because of the overt nature of the game you are playing it builds your confidence and lets you relax too.

I have never seen it taken beyond the rolled-up-sleeves-and-tie stage, but see how far you can go …

For women there's no useful equivalent. It raises too many male expectations. The issue for women is jewellery – and an outfit that gives you somewhere to put a radio microphone without embarrassing the sound man who attaches it to you.

Jewellery looks great under spotlights. It is twice as bright, twice as shiny, twice as effective – and twice as distracting. So a single piece can be effective, but don't overdo it.

As an experienced presenter warns: "There is always a tension between form and content, but as form gets more powerful, the mismatch is becoming more dangerous."

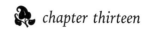 *chapter thirteen*

Snatching Triumph from the Jaws of Disaster

When it all goes wrong

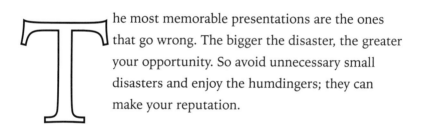The most memorable presentations are the ones that go wrong. The bigger the disaster, the greater your opportunity. So avoid unnecessary small disasters and enjoy the humdingers; they can make your reputation.

Death Wish vs. Hand of God

In presentations there are two sorts of disasters. Those that are self-inflicted – let's call them the 'Death Wish' disasters. And those that aren't – the 'Hand of God'.

'Death Wish' disasters are the result of poor planning, poor judgement, injudicious short-cuts, inappropriate penny-pinching and just plain incompetence. They embarrass speakers, embarrass their hosts and alienate the audience. Such presenters thoroughly deserve all the ignominy and loss of reputation that will befall them.

Avoid such disasters at all costs. All it needs is a little thought and a little planning.

'Hand of God' disasters, on the other hand, start by looking dreadful – the projector expiring in a cloud of black smoke, the power cut plunging the room into darkness, the screen falling down, your worst nightmare happening in front of your very eyes, and worse, in front of your expectant audience.

But what appears to be a disaster becomes one only if you make it so. Fate has conspired to give you a great opportunity and one you will rarely have again. The audience is suddenly wholly on your side and willing you to overcome all obstacles.

The most memorable presentations are always the ones that go wrong.

The most memorable presentations are always the ones that go wrong; and so much the better if they are rescued from disaster by the skill and competence of the presenter. Heroic stuff. And really very easy to pull off.

But two rules.

One: Stay cool, don't lose your nerve.

And two: While you are standing in front of your audience never, never blame other people. Even if it is clearly their fault. You can give them hell later.

Death Wish disasters

Disasters in this category are of three types: disastrous content, disastrous delivery and disastrous logistics.

Disastrous content

1. Misreading the brief

   Remember answering the exam question you thought they'd asked, not the one they did ask? It happens in presentations too.

   While it mainly affects people pitching for business, it has a close cousin – the mis-brief.

   Too often guest speakers, especially the stars, are badly briefed or not briefed at all in the mistaken belief (that they may share) that all they need to do is a 'turn'. Sir Terence Conran, an urbane, thoughtful and accomplished speaker, was invited to give the keynote address to a Bordeaux Wines management conference. It was not a happy experience. Wrong story. Wrong time. Wrong brief. Right mess.

   Wrong story. Wrong time. Wrong brief. **Right mess.**

   So why you are giving the presentation and what is expected of you? Is it for your insight into the subject matter? Or your ability to tell good stories and keep the audience awake after lunch? Are you the first speaker? The last? Are you following on from another speaker or will you be talking after a coffee break? How much time have you been allotted? Does this include questions? Will questions be allowed during the presentation or only at the end?

   Once you have prepared your presentation, go back and re-read the brief. It may surprise you.

2. Misreading the audience

An advertising colleague, a brilliant freelance copywriter, was handling two assignments and rushed in to a meeting late and a little flustered to present creative concepts on children's shoes. After a few minutes he noticed the audience getting a little restless, when he was passed a note by one of the ad agency people. This read: 'Mike, what the hell are you doing? This is not the Shoes client, it's the Nuts client.'

Nothing daunted, he continued to present his advertising ideas for a moment or two, then said: 'Gentlemen, you may be wondering why I am using shoes to illustrate these concepts. But the problems you are facing in the nuts business are complex and I thought it would be helpful to get them in perspective. So now let's look at how we might apply some of the same ideas to your product, nuts ...' He got away with it.

Never take your audience for granted. Who are they? Why are they coming? How many of them? What is their degree of skill, knowledge and experience in your subject? Have they heard you speak before?

3. Getting the structure wrong

Once you have got your head round the subject and the audience, you need to pin down the content and how you will put it across.

There are a couple of useful rules, both as old as the hills. The first, the one we keep coming back to, no apology, is:

Tell a story – with a start, a middle and an end.

Whether you are presenting to a customer, to investors or to your boss, always start structuring your presentation by deciding what is the one big thing that you want them to take away, and what it is you want them to do about it. This will help you develop a narrative line, and a logic to the presentation which will drive remorselessly towards your conclusion. Include whatever supports this; exclude everything else.

The second rule is:

"Tell them what you are going to say, say it, and then tell them what you said."

There are many other ways of structuring a presentation, but this is a pretty good place to start unless you are a highly experienced speaker with your own inimitable style.

4. Confused slides make for confused audiences
Having worked out roughly what you want to say, decide on the visual aids you are going to need. Do you really want a PowerPoint presentation? Or something more exotic? Or simpler? Do you need anything at all?

Once you have decided what slides you do need, do them as well and as simply as possible. Tufte's remark, quoted elsewhere, that 'clear graphics convey clear thinking' is nowhere better demonstrated than in the average cluttered PowerPoint presentation.

Too many presenters confuse what works well on paper with what works well on a screen.

This slide really happened:

> Questions regarding ownership of and access
> to information has been a strong determinant
> of the very new business plans that have
> evolved. It has been difficult to find
> deployable technology that accommodates
> the resulting business plan uncertainty.

There may be nothing wrong with what it says (although personally I still don't understand it) but as a speaker support slide it is a disaster. It is up there on the screen so it must be important, mustn't it. But while the audience is puzzling out the meaning, they are not listening to a word the speaker is saying.

A classic way of making slides confusing is to use fonts that are too small to read easily. You will find that the more senior your audience are, the more likely they are to be older and therefore half-blind, and the harder it will be for them to read any small print.

Another good reason for making slides big, bold and simple.

5. Going live

They tell actors to avoid working with children and animals. Presenters should never work with anything live.

Live links always fail. Live demonstrations always fail.

Live links always fail.
Live demonstrations always fail.

Always.

Set them up by all means. Rehearse them over and over again. But assume that on the day they will fail and always have something else to hand to make your point. And practise using it.

Don't waste your audience's time and patience by struggling. They know it won't work.

In the early days of mobile phones we helped with a press conference that depended on a telephone link to a well-known soccer personality. He was to be interviewed on his mobile while driving up the motorway. It took several minutes to establish the link, and it was tested the day before, with him sitting in his car. Foolproof.

And it worked perfectly on the day. Except that every time he went under a bridge the line failed and he was cut off. They could get him back within a couple of minutes, by which time another bridge was coming up. And another …

Disastrous delivery

Many 'best practice' techniques for business presentations can and should be ignored by academics. Working with a business school professor we came to the following conclusions.

Don't be too slick. Use acetates, not computers. Writing them by hand is OK. Use black and white, not colour (or not much colour). Always have your slides in the wrong order. Make sure they look dusty and scratched as if they have been used many times before. And finally, to really establish your academic credentials, drop them as you go up to speak.

To a business audience this would smack of incompetence. To an academic audience it shows a healthy disregard for production values in a culture where content is king.

Too many business presenters still get delivery wrong. Not simply because they are nervous – many of the best speakers are nervous (just as some actors claim to be physically sick before a performance) – but because they think only about what they want to give, not about what the audience want to receive.

Do you recognize any of these...?

- Speakers who are surprised by their material ...
  Alarming enough for them, but deeply disturbing for the audience ...

- Speakers who decide to control their own slides and then forget to move them on ...
  Then jump through swathes of material in a few seconds to catch up, undermining their arguments and looking inept ...

- Speakers who read out their slides word for word to the audience ...
  Insulting and boring.

- Speakers who read out their slides word for word to the audience while they stand with their back to them ...
  Insulting and boring in spades.

- Speakers who put up a complex slide and fail to explain it ...
  The audience isn't going to be listening to them while they try to make sense of the slide.

- Speakers who just can't stop ...
  No speaker has ever been criticized for finishing too soon.

- Speakers who read word for word from a script ...
  Why does it always sound as if it's been written by a lawyer or an accountant?

- Speakers who jangle the change in their pocket ...
  Boy are they nervous; patently nervous speakers make for nervous audiences and no one enjoys the experience.

- Speakers who are always out of synch with their slides ... And keep apologizing.
  Often ad-libbers carried away by content. Give up worrying and go with the flow. They have.

These are everyday faults. They are mostly caused by lack of preparation, failure to talk *to* the audience, and plain bad manners.

Disastrous logistics

Logistical problems tend to fall into three groups:

1. *Software problems*

Software problems are presentations that don't arrive or don't work or don't look right or don't behave as they should.

Disasters of this nature are always the fault of the presenter.

Such problems should never arise in a presentation that has been properly checked beforehand. 'Properly Checked' means checking on the actual machine that will be used in the show; essential for anything complex like animations or special fonts.

There is also its cousin 'Adequately Checked'. This is fine in known systems where you are doing nothing ambitious.

Avoid its bastard son 'Just A Quick Check'. And the suicidally inclined 'Thought It Would Be OK'.

Avoid its bastard son
'Just A Quick Check'.

Here are some laments you will hear often.

- 'It looks all wrong'

(your presentation may have been copied on to a new template for the show which will override your template; or you're using fonts that aren't on the host computer, including logo fonts).

- 'I e-mailed the presentation hours ago but they can't find it'
  (e-mails were never designed to handle large presentation files and they can take many hours to arrive – assuming that the sender's own system, as well as the recipient's, will even handle files of such size; many are deliberately obstructed by firewalls and other machinations of IT departments).

- 'It's on this disk but your computer can't read it'
  (are you trying to use a Mac disc on a PC?).

- 'It's here on my laptop but they can't transfer it to the computer that's running the show'
  (the file may simply be too big to transfer easily).

- 'All my bullet points have changed'
  (check that you are both using the same version of PowerPoint).

- 'None of the sound effects work'

- 'The animations run too fast/too slow/don't run at all'

- 'The video doesn't work'
  (you're in a very technical area here – you need to make sure that the necessary audio/video drivers are on the 'show' computer, and that they are of a similar or later date than your own; and if you are using animations, that the right software is installed – certain animations will only run on current versions of PowerPoint).

  It is so much simpler to check well in advance.

2. *Hardware problems*
Hardware problems are typified by equipment that doesn't arrive or doesn't work or doesn't behave as the presenter thinks it should.

It can start with your own computer. Make sure that it is compatible with the projection equipment (particularly resolution and refresh rate). You may need to reset it. Do you know how?

With proper planning you should rarely meet with hardware problems in big set-piece presentations with professional support or in purpose-built presentation suites with proper management. But equipment, however well maintained, can still fail without warning and accidents genuinely do happen.

Yes but ...

Increasingly as equipment gets lighter and more portable, a do-it-yourself attitude is starting to take hold: plug-in and go, it's easy. Power to the people, and so on.

At the DIY level the standard problems are:

- Leads between the computer and projector are damaged or aren't long enough, aren't correct or aren't there.

- There is no power socket near enough or there aren't enough of them and there are no extension power blocks.

- The computer doesn't automatically switch through to the projector, or when it does the picture is a mess.

- The room lighting is too bright or too dark and there's nothing in between.

- You didn't bring any audio connectors for your computer.

- How do I run my video tape? (PAL or NTSC? BetaSP or VHS? analogue or digital?...)

If you plan to run a DIY show it is best to use your own equipment that can be set up properly in advance. And always carry a spares kit, including extension leads, perhaps in the boot of your car.

Never trust what is on site, whatever reassurances you may be given. Always check in good time that what you have works. And always make sure you know who is in charge of the equipment and how to contact them (ideally get them to meet you when you arrive).

The range of possible hardware problems is infinitely long. Much longer than the list of hardware itself.

Microphones that fail or 'ring' when you don't have a proper sound system or an engineer who can use it.

Projectors that don't project whatever button you press.

Lighting that fails or gets in your eyes when the camera crew insist that it must be that way otherwise they can't film you.

The computer that doesn't connect – wrong leads, wrong connector, wrong interface.

The power failure that takes down all the equipment; or the partial failure ('brownout') that causes everything to flicker but crashes the computer (so use a laptop).

It's too dark to read your script.

The lectern is too high or too low for comfort, and too rickety to lean on.

The support materials (handouts) don't appear in time ('yes, the taxi left here ages ago'; 'they might be in the post-room …').

Backups fail (you do have backups, don't you?).

Sometimes the technicians screw up. This is most likely in my experience when there is an in-house team working with a group of outside technicians. The role of the producer is then critical.

Even the compère can screw up. Reginald Bosanquet, the co-presenter of ITV's *News at Ten*, was brilliant in this role, a real pro. Despite sometimes being on his second bottle of

Chablis by 10am. In our experience he never got it wrong, but as you watched him, knowing what you did, it definitely added a certain *frisson* to the occasion.

3. *Venue problems*

Venue problems mostly occur where the venue is grossly inappropriate for the presentation in the first place.

We once had to link two small rooms for a meeting in a London hotel, on different floors and at opposite ends of an old, straggling building. Each cable run was 500 metres, in and out of rooms, down corridors, through windows, across roofs. Not only were there numerous technical issues to be solved, but it took the crew several extra hours just to get the wiring in place and tested.

Other common problems include poor access, noise from adjacent rooms, lack of control of lighting, lack of window blinds, poor sound system (*never* trust hotel sound systems unless you can test them properly first).

Backing up a presentation

As a presenter, you will of course always have a backup copy of your presentation; on disk if it is under about 1Mb and otherwise on CD-Rom. Depending on your level of paranoia, you may also have it on 35mm slides and acetates.

Now think what you would do if there was a power cut so none of these worked. Would you give up and go home? Or (assuming that the emergency lighting had come on) would you talk to the audience without your visuals? Good. That is the ultimate backup. It also shows that there is Life Without PowerPoint.

Is it worth the cost of backing up?

If you are concerned about how much resource is appropriate to a presentation, just work out roughly the cost of the time of the people you are presenting to, the cost of their travel, and so on. Add them all up and work out how much of it would be wasted if your presentation were to fail. Then look again at the budget for your presentation. Particularly the investment in backup equipment.

Hand of God disasters

There are times when, despite all your care, attention, planning and other best efforts, something goes disastrously wrong. We were running a show for 500 people at a London theatre and we were using a big, expensive projector. We had used it many times before and it was regarded as the best in the business.

But just in case (and taking our own advice), we had a backup. Not a cheap, second-best projector, but the full monty – a duplicate.

We had duplicated everything. All in place the previous day, all fully checked and tested. And the theatre had recently installed a sophisticated power management system, so only an Act of God could bring the power down.

only an Act of God could bring the power down

It did.

First the main projector went. Ten seconds later the backup went. Unheard of. The projectors were checked and found to be fault-free. And the power system was fine. The cause was technically very interesting but as far as the presenter was concerned, she was standing in front of an expectant audience with her dignity, not to mention her credibility, on the line. She knew something had gone wrong, but neither she, nor we, knew what, or how long it would take to fix.

There was plenty of controlled panic back-stage as we tried to work out how to get the show back on the road. But Marjorie Scardino stayed completely calm. She indicated that there was a technical hitch as if such problems were completely understandable and only to be expected, and switched to a Q&A session. Once everything was working again, she resumed where she had left off. It was the best of a series of presentations that she gave that day.

It is interesting to look at why this was successful. By staying calm she looked in control of herself and her material; had she become flustered it would quickly have unsettled the audience.

She was polite to the technicians, commenting only 'I'm sure they'll have this fixed in a minute', which showed belief and trust in her team, another positive message. Had she panicked and bawled them out she would have caused even more problems back-stage and looked shrill and grudging to her audience.

By switching to something unscheduled but meaningful and useful, she turned a negative situation into a positive one, making for a better audience experience and enhancing her reputation.

If you know where you are **trying to go** when disaster strikes, **you can still get there.**

Gordon Owen, Chairman of Energis, recounts an experience with 35mm slides.

66At Cable and Wireless we used a set of 35mm slides for four major presentations on the same morning. The order of the slides during the first show was quite wrong and this was changed for the second show. The order was still wrong, and wrong for the third and fourth shows too, but each time the slides came up in a quite different order. It taught me a lot about flexibility and not getting too hung up when things go wrong.99

Recently a carefully prepared and rehearsed keynote presentation to an audience flown in from the USA appeared to have gone disastrously wrong when the in-house projector failed just as the speaker stood up to begin.

Hoping that the technicians would somehow save the day he resorted to describing his first slide, then talked to it. Then he described the second, elaborating a little. And so on, until the invisible graphics were as fanciful and mouthwatering as anything on a master chef's exotic menu.

The audience were drawn in to the game and the presentation was a great success. Like good radio the mental images carried the day.

The projector never did work.

I have been in halls plunged into darkness as the hired generator failed; evacuated from buildings mid-presentation when a fire alarm went off; forced to set up equipment without a crew when a City church tower crashed to the ground and brought London to a standstill; supplied battery-driven loudhailers as backup for an AGM in case the building was bombed and the presentation had to move to the open air.

The more presentations you do, the more you will have similar tales to tell.

But always,
the show must go on.

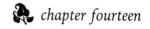 *chapter fourteen*

TAMING THE TECHNICIANS

Conferences and how to survive them

Plugging into conferences

You arrive to give your speech at a major conference. Every facility has been promised, every door will be opened. But when you arrive there are 30 other speakers all trying to sort out their presentations for the eight morning streams. There has been a technical breakdown and nobody seems to know where to send you or what to do. You've got a CD which includes sound and video. The timing of the various links is critical. And you want to link to your web site to download some extra stuff.

What are your chances?

Frankly, pretty poor. Have you checked the technical standards in advance? Have you been in the evening before and done a technical rehearsal? Have you checked that they can run sound and video (your sort of video) on their computer? That they have all the right drivers? Did you send them a CD for testing? Have they got your fonts on their system (your exact fonts, not some with the same name that are pretty close)?

Unless you can check on everything in a sensible way, always take a laptop as backup, on which your presentation is known to run correctly. And never trust a conference (or anyone else for that matter) to let you display a live web site as part of your presentation.

More than anything else, work on the principle that if it can go wrong, it will.

Creating the right environment

Although the hired hall with rented equipment is becoming less attractive as equipment (particularly projector) prices fall and in-house or specialist facilities flourish, good sound and lighting remain as important as ever.

Many speakers hate stage lighting – it gets in their eyes and prevents them seeing their audience properly. The better and brighter the projector, the higher the general lighting levels can be and the less disconcerting the spotlights will seem.

In deciding on the lighting levels, decide on your key audience. If the live audience in front of you is your key audience, with recordings being done 'for the record' or occasional web viewing, then ignore the pleas of the lighting engineers and go for a modest level of lighting that lets you communicate comfortably within the room. You do need a certain basic level of lighting to make you look human.

You do need a certain basic level of lighting to make **you look human.**

But if the live audience is there only to bring life to the recording – a studio audience – then suffer whatever the lighting engineers throw at you. Their job is to make you look great and the recording look great and you should let them do it.

Sound is pretty straightforward. Beware of situations where people in the front row ask questions without a microphone, so those at the back can't hear. Either get them to use a microphone or repeat the question. Otherwise it looks as if you are having a private conversation with a few cronies.

Managing equipment

Portable equipment is now mostly inexpensive, simple and reliable.

Faults are almost always down to wires and connectors, which are the things most often maltreated by people in a hurry. Wires get trodden on, snagged, yanked, jerked, pulled, knotted and worse. Treat them as a sailor would a rope. Coil wires with a half twist. Look after them. Love them. Wires are your link with the audience.

Connectors suffer the same fate – jammed on, screwed down at the wrong angle, forced on, forced off. They contain a series of delicate pins, and if one breaks, so does your presentation.

Technical teams and how to survive them

Use experienced people and brief them properly – not just on your audio-visual requirements but on the purpose and tenor of the meeting. Don't buy the cheapest solution, buy the right one for the job – the money you might save is minimal in comparison with the cost of problems.

When you meet the crew in the morning they often grunt a lot and you may get a false impression of their commitment and enthusiasm. Remember, they've probably been up all night, working for you. They've got a long day ahead too, mostly spent in hot, dark and uncomfortable conditions while you drone on. It isn't an easy job.

And at the end, try not to be too busy to thank them. Not enough people do.

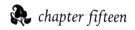 *chapter fifteen*

PRESENTING INTO THE FUTURE

Where is all this technology taking us?

Curiously, technology is the least of the issues except in one respect.

The computer allows us to review and hone and redraft our presentations and speeches in a way we could never do before. For those of us who do a lot of speeches, the process of 'polishing' has become far more exacting in time and effort than the original construction.

What's really changed is that presentations have become a norm.

We live in a world of perpetual pitches. For contracts, for promotion, for keeping one's job (daily). I even once reflected, somewhat satirically, on the idea of having to repitch your marriage.

Imagine your spouse saying:

66Darling. There's something you should know.
I'm reviewing our marriage and putting it up to pitch.
As incumbent, you, of course, should have nothing to worry
about ...99

We are entering a world where the presentation will replace the essay in the academic world. A world where organizing information into a coherent format – a presentation – is something everyone aspires to.

Imagine if all the best advice in this book was absorbed by everyone. The next decade or so would be full of bank managers presenting to us and vice versa, of much more didactic (and probably better) TV programmes, of employees saying not 'could I have a few minutes ...?' but 'can I present to you?'. Seduction would comprise a laptop presentation starting 'Sexual Overview'. The future is rich in presentational promise.

But technology will make the future even richer. Presentations will become less boring. Layouts will improve. Software such as 'Lessmore' (I've made it up) will edit over-wordy presentations and throw in suggestions – 'Try something dramatic here ... Lessmore detects tempo fade.'

And just as the Americans seem inveterate users of therapists, virtually all executives will employ limited but consistent third party advice to help them improve:

- self-projection
- self-confidence
- focus
- empathy
- dramatic skill.

One day everyone will be competent and many will be great.

One day everyone will be competent and many will be great.

We shall then move to a new chapter: 'Deconstructing the presentation.' But that's some way off right now.

Presentations are such a major part of business that they will be continually scrutinized for ways to become better, more efficient, more productive.

So how will the presentation stars of 2010 woo their audiences? How will they seduce, inveigle and win?

Look back to the nineties – 35mm slides, acetates, 'decks', flipcharts, computers starting to be useful but a nightmare linking them to projectors.

Go back to the early eighties, and it's still not much different from the nineties (Apple IIs on large monitors for those of us pushing at the edges).

Presentations have always been about people talking to an audience, and clarifying what they are saying with the help of simple visual aids.

So has nothing changed?

The key difference is that in 1980 the visual aids were the last part of the chain, the thing you did when you had the presentation nailed down. They were simply too complicated, too slow and too expensive to change.

Now they are often the first thing to be done. They capture the argument as it develops; they can be printed, e-mailed and circulated with ease, amended time and time again at little or no cost; above all, they help speakers fine-tune their presentation.

They have become the fundamental working tool, not just the end-result.

the fundamental working tool, not just the end-result

Presentation software such as PowerPoint is full of bells and whistles, animations, transitions and effects, but these are mostly minor distractions. Visual aids are basically simple devices.

From this perspective, in 2010 we can expect more to be the same than different. More bells, perhaps. More whistles. But a live audience in a room with a speaker at a lectern.

Talking, listening, watching.

That's the lesson from history.

But history can be a poor basis for predicting the future. Remember the forecasts in the 1890s that rising levels of horse manure would bring cities worldwide to a standstill within 20 years?

So what does technology tell us?

Computers will undoubtedly get faster, smaller, lighter. Laptops will play high-quality music, show films and TV programmes, and run your bath for you when you are on your way home. Some of this may be useful to presenters, particularly the bath.

And while it may well be possible to run presentations from your mobile phone or organizer or fountain pen, these will not seriously affect the presentation process.

Presentation files will get bigger and more complex – they are already getting too big to be handled by many e-mail systems and it is often quicker to courier a large presentation across town than e-mail it. Suddenly we are moving backwards again.

Broadband promises to rescue us. A revolution? Or just the same old things a little bigger, better and faster?

Television is going digital, and its techniques and capabilities are starting to appear on computers.

This opens up a host of opportunities to presenters – live video backgrounds; zooming into ever more detailed maps; running several computers at once to create composite displays; page curl transitions; live links with presenters elsewhere in the world. And so on. Just like TV in fact.

In ten years all this will happen, with nothing more complicated for you to worry about than an icon on your laptop. Or organizer. Or phone. Or …

But.

And there's a big but.

> The ability of software to do extraordinary things is undermined by **the inability of most executives** to make it part of their day-to-day experience.

The ability of software to do extraordinary things is undermined by the inability of most executives to make it part of their day-to-day experience. They simply won't have the time, or the skills.

The story of Dwight Cavendish's laser projector illustrates the pitfalls of technology. Developed in the eighties, watching *Star Wars* projected on to the side of a barn in broad daylight was stunning – you could even measure the scan lines with a ruler, they were so bright, crisp and clear. Overwhelming. Self-evidently the future.

But such projectors were big, complex, and needed plumbing into the mains water supply. At a venue in Germany during a comfort interval, so many toilets were flushed simultaneously that the water pressure dropped and the projector went up in smoke.

The highest technology.
But not toilet trained.

These days 'audio-visual' often means an ever proliferating tangle of cables. Soon everything should link together without wires.

Technology is also changing the distribution of presentations, mainly through the web and related technologies. This in turn is changing what can be done with presentations and how they are used.

You can already display your presentation in several venues at the same time. So you can be speaking in New York, and your colleagues in London can follow your presentation through the web, complete with an audio and video link if necessary, all from your laptop. Of course, if you move out of range of the tiny camera built in, no one will be able to see you; and if you stray away from the microphone, no one can hear you. But within reason, and provided you stay rooted to the spot, you should be OK.

A bit like the old days of videoconferencing.

Of course, it can also be done very well with today's technology, but that involves technicians, equipment and a fair amount of money. Soon it will be possible to do it pretty adequately (if you're not too ambitious) for the price of a phone call.

Aye, there's the rub. Almost everything you will be able to do in ten years' time can already be done today, at a price. What you pay for today is sophistication and hands-on professionalism. What you will get by waiting ten years is DIY. For some this will seem like liberation; for others it will just add to the worry and the list of all the things that might go wrong.

You can of course already put your presentation on to your web site for people to view at their leisure though this hardly counts as giving a presentation. But as the quality improves, you will look worse. Not better, worse.

But as the quality improves, you will look worse. Not better, worse.

Viewers will no longer be amazed that they can see you at all; they will start to criticize your style, your delivery, your dress sense, even your arguments.

The web is the public. They're used to TV standards. Anything that falls short will look unprofessional. That's you.

This will put a premium on presentation skills. It will expose them, not hide them. As Charles Rosner says elsewhere, 'The cost of making the top man look good in presentations is escalating fast.'

So apart from a few stars, business will continue to be driven by face-to-face presentations and discussions simply because they are innately more effective and flexible, and can focus more on content and less on delivery.

So will nothing change?

Yes. There's a generation of school leavers entering business who will start to change these rules. They have a visual imagination honed on Playstations, Rugrats, Ali G and pop promos. For them, the shorter the sound bite, the more intelligible it is. It's a visual world and it moves fast. Today's presentations will seem ineffably prosaic and boring.

They will throw a multitude of images at you, will handle

These youngsters will want to stimulate minds, want you to feel as well as consider.

sound and video with ease, and attempt to drive you towards a conclusion.

Some will do it badly, some brilliantly. Much like today's presenters in fact.

They will start to break down barriers.

Will this be more effective? Who knows. It is not a classical, forensic, analytical approach to problem solving. It is not the way business has ever argued its case.

But will it speak to their own generation? Undoubtedly.

You can glimpse what's coming: watch *Top of the Pops* and pop promos. Some advertising for youth products is already adapting. Look at how ten-years-olds use mobile phones and how they have hijacked and reinvented short text messaging for their own ends.

This is multi-layer communication. It is undisciplined and anarchic. It revels in short-cuts, oblique references and imagery which is out of date almost before it has become mainstream.

It will of course calm down, even stabilise before it hits business. But hit it, it will.

That's the future.

Inspirers, Perspirers, Aspirers

part three

❧

Interviews with master presenters

Going down like a lead balloon
Colin Prescot, Chief Executive, Flying Pictures

❧

The changing face of the salesman
Paul Barratt, Sales Representative, Gaskell Carpet Tiles

❧

Discipline, focus and audience centricity
Chris Milburn, Head of Investor Relations, Centrica plc

❧

Yes Minister
Two senior civil servants

❧

Being a Baroness and a Knight at the same time
Baroness Knight of Collingtree, DBE

❧

It's getting better all the time
Kaizo Public Relations

❧

Well thought-out conversations
Simon Walker, Communications Secretary to Her Majesty The Queen

Colin Prescot
Going down like a lead balloon

Colin Prescot is something of a one-off. An urbane old Etonian who is disarmingly self-effacing, he runs a profitable company, Flying Pictures, with a balance sheet many CEOs would envy. He performs extraordinary feats of aerial daring (the Royal Aero club awarded him a coveted Gold Medal for his 18-day world endurance record for any aircraft in the Earth's atmosphere) and he's written an amazing book, *To the Edge of Space*, which is both exciting and very funny.

So do presentations matter to someone who just two years ago spent almost three weeks in a capsule under a balloon up to 30,000 feet above the Earth without any form of control – no accelerator, no steering, no brakes? Surely a boardroom seems a prosaic place for a would-be astronaut?

Colin is a pragmatist, however.

66 **You don't get £2.5m in sponsorship money without doing a lot of presentations.**

I love doing them and I love visual aids.

Talking to pictures is always exciting, explaining what's going on, what lies behind the simple image. 99

I love doing them and
I love visual aids.

He also explains with greater clarity than most the sheer, breathtaking uncertainty of the presentation.

66 **Like ballooning, it all depends on which way the wind is blowing.** 99

He describes one of those oddities we've all experienced. Exactly one week apart he made two speeches to similar audiences, the British Airship and Balloon Clubs of, respectively, London and the West. These were in part promotional exercises for his book.

These speeches – well-rehearsed and done many times before – always go down well. But the London one was an exception. It went down brilliantly. Laughter. Applause. And what's more, the sale of books was 1.5 per member of the audience.

Bristol was also an exception. It went down as Colin put it 'like a lead balloon'. No laughter, except when improvizing in desperation but also because by then he felt it to be true:

It went down as Colin put it 'like a lead balloon'.

66 Let's face it, all balloonists are tossers. 99

and book sales at 0.04 per member of the audience.

What, I asked, went wrong?

Colin was mystified but said with some vehemence:

66 Presentations with visual aids and a relatively formal setting are one thing anyone can be reasonably competent at. Speeches are for pros and I'm an amateur (most of us are). 99

The theory I advanced is the simplistic one that positive audience response always enhances performance, and vice versa, and to an acute degree with those who are less comfortable with public performances.

positive audience response always enhances performance, and vice versa

Thus:

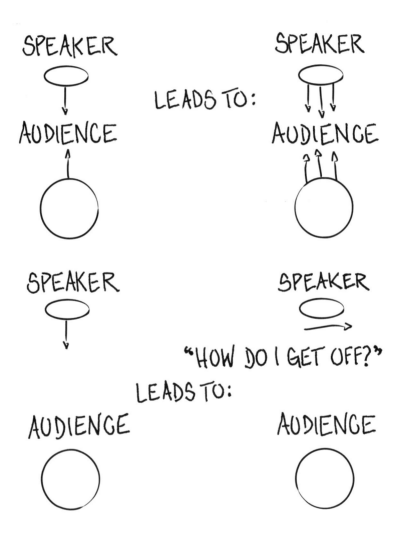

Colin studied this with interest, agreed it was probably right and added:

66 **But it's a complete load of bollocks – you've either got it or you haven't.** 99

Subsequently he learned there had been a problem with the Bristol sound system which made him difficult to hear.

He then told the story of Christopher Bailey who celebrated his 50th birthday in fine fashion in Los Angeles. A large crowd turned out to his boozy dinner, after which he made the most brilliant, funny but really quite long speech.

He sat down to rapturous applause and as his guests wiped their eyes they were horrified to hear the toastmaster announce yet another speaker (they really were all 'laughed out').

The new speaker stood and surveyed his audience, who were staring apprehensively at his large sheaf of notes.

He paused, then said: 'Nah, I can't follow that ...!' and on all fours went back to his seat.

Biggest applause of the evening.

Proof again that less is more.

Paul Barratt
The changing face of the salesman

Paul Barratt is 23. Recently graduated with a management degree from UMIST, he works as a sales representative for Gaskell Carpet Tiles. His patch is Greater London.

And he loves his job. Like so many of the refreshing young people nowadays he is hugely, bright-eyedly ambitious. He believes he'll be very wealthy one day running his own business.

In the meantime he's professionally attacking a very traditional market where a variety of influences are brought to bear on any sale. What the architect says, what the clerk of works thinks, what the wholesaler wants, who the specifier is. The sale of a carpet tile is a Byzantine process.

The sale of a carpet tile is a Byzantine process.

Anyone who's been a salesman knows the score. It's about relationships. It's about scratching backs. The best jokes (and the worst language) come out of sales meetings. Sophistication is subsumed by a kind of laddism. True for Heinz, IBM or Gaskell.

Yet Paul is uncertain this is right.

66 I want to do more sophisticated presentations to my customers. 99

This is like Billy Elliott. Salesmen don't aspire to presentations any more than Geordies do ballet. Dangerously counter cultural, although with people like Paul around this is changing.

Why does he want to do presentations?

Because it makes the process more serious.

Because it imposes focus. Focus on business issues, not extraneous stuff.

Because it makes customers think. Think about what they need.

Because it's professional.

The vision of a thinking salesforce driven to use the device of presentations to distil and to focus on business issues is impressive.

Most impressive, perhaps, is Paul's realization that for most of us being a stand-up comic alone is not enough in modern business.

being a stand-up comic alone is not enough in modern business

IBM were the presentation wizards of the seventies.

In the future no one will get fired for buying on the back of a thoughtfully constructed business-like presentation either.

Maybe the real power of the presentation process is yet to manifest itself – at the sales coalface.

Chris Milburn
Discipline, focus and audience centricity

Chris Milburn is Head of Investor Relations at Centrica plc and a past Chairman of the Investor Relations Society. He attests immediately to the importance of presentations:

❝The time that the CEO and CFO are prepared to invest in presentations has increased considerably.❞

He sees management as recognizing that they have to identify the important points and focus on them and that audiences too are better and more appreciative of open and cooperative management. The trick is to find the right balance between formal content and open discussion.

The right balance between formal content and open discussion.

Centrica has been turned around since the mid-nineties and is now highly regarded in the City.

❝Four years ago we were trying to underpin a survival strategy. The business has changed substantially and the way it communicates has changed with it.❞

❝It has been a sequence of communication exercises and presentations where we have tried to keep the analyst community as informed and up to date as possible as our strategy has developed.

The strength of presentations is that they let us get a clear message over quickly to a defined group. A presentation demands that the speaker 'owns' the strategy, and that's very important.

Seminars, on the other hand, provide background information and understanding and give us the chance to show our strength in depth. **”**

He is emphatic that content alone is not enough:

“The need to present well is critical, especially to external audiences. We have developed a culture of openness and sincerity and genuinely try to establish productive relationships with our audiences. **”**

Chris recalls the days of design departments and 35mm slides.

“PowerPoint is much more flexible. We use and reuse existing presentations, cutting and pasting material to quickly create new presentations. **”**

But there are drawbacks:

“You need to make sure you can verify information and check statements if they are detached from their original context. **”**

The importance of major presentations is well recognized throughout the company. Once a schedule is drawn up, key speakers clear their diaries and nothing is left to chance.

“This way the presentation is properly polished, the arguments (and emphasis) are well thought through, and there is greater familiarity with the content, to ensure that it is genuinely 'owned' by the speakers. This, in turn, makes for a better Q&A session. **”**

There is nothing easy about creating a presentation, particularly where complex or technical issues need to be explained to a non-technical audience.

“It can take a full week to create just one or two slides on a ticklish subject. **”**

It can take a **full week** to create just one or **two slides on a ticklish subject.**

As to the future, Chris makes five key points:

1. The Internet will become more central as wide disclosure becomes important, but companies must still remain open in the way they respond to analysts and investors.

2. It is difficult to communicate complex messages widely. But this can't be ducked as at the same time we want the market to be transparent.

3. Personal contact mustn't be compromised by technology. We must never let ourselves get hidden away.

4. Videoconferencing is simply not a good enough substitute for live presentations. It can foreground presentation skills at the expense of content.

5. You have to find the right medium for the message.

Finally, Chris reflects on the importance of presentations:

66 **When things become formalized in presentations, it makes you think them through, it makes you more disciplined.** 99

Yes Minister

Two civil servants, both at the top of their respective departments, spoke to us. In preserving their anonymity we are merely following accepted practice and allowing ourselves a little more licence in interpreting their remarks.

Whitehall, in common with the rest of the world, is a PowerPoint-packed zone, especially among younger civil servants.

But paper continues to fill all ministers' lives.

66 **This is an ordered culture – decisions must be *seen* to be soundly based, which means an audit trail is desirable. This in turn means more paper. And it's getting worse, not better.** 99

Yet the crude reality of ministerial life is one of chaos – meetings cancelled at short notice, political imperatives intruding on affairs of state, too much to do, too little time and, especially, too little sleep. Much of the work is done in cars or at weekends.

No room for PowerPoint there.

But there's good stuff going on. Transcriptions from public enquiries available in real time and on the web too. And there are horror stories.

There was a major presentation by the Ministry of Defence at 10 Downing Street. This is not a media-friendly place (and that is not a comment about the Prime Minister's then Press Spokesman Alastair Campbell but about the facilities available). Being conscientious (and we should be grateful they are), the chaps from the MOD brought two computers and two projectors to the meeting. For some reason neither system could be made to work.

Even this might not have been a disaster because they had taken the precaution of bringing backup prints. But the whole presentation was structured around 'redstream' activity and 'yellowstream' activity. Sadly the printouts were only in black and white ...

As this civil servant urbanely observed:

Well, you only get one chance.

Everyone nowadays is talking about the need for 'snappier' presentations, but it is clear that, despite journalists' obsession with contemporary governments being more focused on style than substance, civil servants are very 'content' focused.

66 We try to make presentations simple, not complex … clearly showing what's going on and trying to influence thinking (actually getting people to think). We have a slight cultural aversion to pretty packaging. 99

Yet this tells only part of the story. Cut through the practised urbanity and you find some very streetwise people who shrewdly assess the tools of the trade. They know the value of what is said depends as much on timing as on the content itself. Rightly they don't like their flexibility locked into a computer. Impossible not to be impressed by their sheer mastery of their respective subjects.

They know the value of what is said depends as much on timing as on the content itself.

It is clear that in the world of *realpolitik*

66 presentations will never become central to the interface between civil service and ministers. 99

(That's civil service speak for 'Get yourself on to their political radar screen and they're a captive audience – more a case of cabaret than theatre'.)

But as civil servants communicate increasingly with other constituencies, the quality of presentation will become more important – Treasury presentations are already regarded as ahead of the pack. Presentation training is now part of the ethos, although older and more senior civil servants view this trendy trend with a degree of ironic weariness.

What has changed is technology.

66 **Ten years ago we'd have had to choose between full dress slides or an informal talk. Now we can do a ten-minute PowerPoint presentation. But beware of too much sophistication; you ruin impact by having technical hiccoughs.** 99

The **constant emphasis** on content and argument **is refreshing.**

From the private sector tendency of:

66 **It's not what you say, it's the way that you say it.** 99

to:

66 **It's absolutely and entirely what you say. And when you say it.** 99

And, whisper it who dares, these are deeply bright, war-scarred professionals who are often the best presenters in the business. They just don't like to admit it.

Baroness Knight of Collingtree
Being a Baroness and a Knight at the same time – a presentational coup

We met in the Royal Gallery at the House of Lords, which must be one of the most impressive meeting rooms anywhere. It's where heads of state speak on formal occasions and its only disadvantage is the distraction of so much opulence and so much history. And a certain lack of power points.

Jill Knight was a leading Conservative and MP for Edgbaston, Birmingham, for 31 years from 1966. She is now Baroness Knight of Collingtree and a Member of the Council of Europe, but she remains as enthusiastic and committed a parliamentarian as ever.

66Visual aids are against the rules of the House and people have been severely rebuked for using them. This does not prevent members improvizing – waving newspaper headlines or holding up a packet of cigarettes to emphasize their point.99

So visual aids will out, it seems. They are simply too useful and natural a mechanism for punctuating rhetoric and emphasizing critical points.

66In my constituency I often found a shopping basket useful.99

They say Margaret Thatcher used to handbag her adversaries. A shopping basket sounds a much more formidable weapon.

Jill was 13 when she decided she wanted to be a politician and she took every chance to speak in public. She says that not all politicians are good speakers, but if they want to be successful they had better jolly well learn to be. And the only way to learn is by doing it. And doing it. And doing it.

She also had stage training and earned her living for a short time acting and singing, a pretty good preparation for the political arena and the media spotlight.

She notes that political speeches are different from business speeches because politicians are not just selling mousetraps.

political speeches are different from business speeches

66I think one of the differences between a politician and a salesman is that a politician has at any moment to draw on a huge range of knowledge. A salesman is much more focused.

Visual aids help the salesman because they narrow down and focus the point of discussion. This is not often the point of a political speech. Politicians are often more interested in propositions; we're usually looking at the wider context. 99

Politicians, she says, are always conscious of how the press will react, and to be effective you need to know what they will seize on. But no politician can control this process. (Intriguingly, in a world where business becomes of greater account, that is exactly how CEOs see their role.)

She is no fan of the way Parliament has changed, saying the way the House is organized now does nothing to improve political oratory. Fewer politicians attend each debate and this inevitably lessens their quality.

66In any form of speaking, a good line is still very powerful. I remember describing some colleagues on one committee as having 'hearts as big as buckets and brains as big as peas'.

Such phrases do catch your attention. When they are apt they strike a chord and can stick in your mind for years. 99

Like all politicians it's the whiff of napalm in the morning that does it for Jill.

66 **Good elections are always lively. Your aim isn't to show that you know all the answers but that you do understand all the problems and want to solve them.**

If I didn't have an answer I would always ask for a name and address and offer to reply later. And I always did. Promises, in politics as anywhere else, must be kept.

The battle with your opponent in an election should never be personal. I would never argue on a personal level. 99

Jill represents a strong tradition in English politics; but sadly, most of us would see politics as becoming increasingly, and to its detriment, personal. There is an increasing trend to the black arts of manipulation; spin and presentation now increasingly come as second nature.

And however strongly the Baroness believes that politicians keep their promises, research from the Henley Centre shows that hardly anyone in the electorate now believes that they do.

But in a bigger sense she is right. Effective presentation is not just about form and content. In the long run it is also about the actions you take or your audience believe you will take. The big lesson from politics is that in the short term presentation may be everything, but that ultimately without follow up action it is nothing.

66 **Speechmaking is about figuring out your audience – you obviously treat OAPs differently from a group of sixth formers. The speech must have its highs and lows, not just a single level, and a touch of humour doesn't go amiss.**

My motto was always 'make 'em think, make 'em laugh, make 'em vote Conservative."

The biggest disasters she can think of have involved misunderstandings due to language.

There was a famous occasion when a delegation went to Albania and after every official engagement the vote of thanks would be given, in rotation, by one of the delegates. Because everything was interpreted, these speeches were kept short and to the point. When it fell to a northern MP to thank his hosts for an excellent tour of the ball-bearing factory and the meal that followed, he spoke in broad Yorkshire (to the consternation of the interpreter – and Jill does broad Yorkshire wonderfully), thanked his hosts profusely and finished with an intended joke – that the only thing missing on the entire trip was crumpets.

Oh the danger of
translated jokes!

Firstly the interpreter was dismayed and ran off to get a dictionary, then his hosts were devastated. Early next morning a plane was sent to Heathrow with a junior diplomat on board to buy crumpets and returned the same day. So the problem appeared to be solved.

Only it led to a worse one. The Albanians had no idea what you do with crumpets. But from that day onwards the delegation had crumpets at every meal. They had roast crumpet. Boiled crumpet. Baked crumpet. Fried crumpet ...

Humour doesn't travel well, Jill notes (better than crumpet, we hope).

KAIZO
'It's getting better, it's getting better all the time'

When The Beatles wrote this, it's improbable they'd ever heard of Kaizen, the Japanese concept of continuous improvement. Kaizo, the UK public relations consultancy – in its own turn based on Kaizen – had not yet been founded.

Whenever I have a meeting I'm presenting and nearly all my life is spent in meetings.

We spoke to the top team there and the universal conclusion was that virtually *all* their time was devoted to presenting.

The art and the anguish of presenting was keenly felt by the whole group, who acknowledged that it was tiring.

66 **Because you spend your time not just talking but listening too …**

You have to listen so you can pick out the 'hot buttons' (it's a bit like being a TV presenter with an earpiece through to the control room). 99

All confessed to having or having had stage fright, especially when presenting to larger groups, and one had seen someone else (thankfully from another company) completely lose it. She began to lose her way and then completely panicked, screeching at her audience:

66 **Stop looking at me … stop looking at me like that … I feel like a rabbit in the headlights.** 99

Yet another proved the perils of the interactive presentation. He (a 'he' this time) was a client who, trying to spice up his highly scripted and carefully visually aided presentation by an early lightness of touch, invited his audience to describe the business they were *really* in. He expected little response, allowing him to demonstrate the answer to his question in glorious technicolour. To his surprise and growing horror the audience shouted back animated answers for a full five minutes and, as they did so, covered every single point in his presentation, rendering him and his presentation redundant.

He had to be led trembling from the stage.

We talked about nervous tension and how it heightened performance.

It's the buzz ...

more than one person said and all agreed there was simply no feeling in life better (OK, maybe one) than the post presentation glow.

66 That sense of energy and exhilaration ... the sense that people love and respect you too ... it's when you surprise yourself and get that amazing adrenalin hangover. 99

Ken Deeks, the Deputy CEO, spoke animatedly about pre- and post-presentational tension. He is a cross between the funniest stand-up comedian you've ever seen and a serious tell-it-from-the-heart business guru. He is mobile, a raconteur and master of the long pause. Surprisingly, he confesses to self-doubt and the terrors (don't all great presenters?). Overcoming the terrors generates the power, he thinks.

66 It's all about getting revved up ... but it's those first few minutes ... I must, absolutely must, get off to a good start. 99

Preparation is key to some and not to others. There really are no rules, it's whatever makes the performer work best, but all described at least one horror story of busking it.

66 **If you're unprepared, there's nowhere to go if it starts to go wrong... I have to know what lies behind the slides and be absolute mistress of the argument.** 99

So everyone felt strongly that being in charge was important. Dreadful to arrive late, not to have done basic reconnaissance of the room, where you are speaking from, and so on.

And the key motive for presenting? In the communications business, Crispin Manners, CEO, was very clear as to the prime motive and motivation.

66 **It's all about winning ... the hardest thing in life is to get people to say 'yes'. Effective presentations create an affirmative atmosphere.** 99

The team at Kaizo summarized the keys to great presentations:

- You've got to create *involvement*.
- You've got to have understanding (audience and speaker – odd how many speakers don't seem to understand what they're saying).
- And you (the speaker) have got to have *belief*. If you don't believe in what you're saying, it shows.

And the 'I wishes'.

66 I wish I was less nervous before the big one. 99

66 I wish I had more time. 99

66 I wish people would discuss rather than just be an audience. 99

❝I wish I had more help. There must be loads of advice that would make me better.❞

❝I wish I did more of this.❞

This?

'Yes, *talking* about it.'

Simon Walker
Well thought-out conversations

Simon Walker is the Queen's Communications Secretary. His office in Buckingham Palace is, by any standards, regal. In the background we hear martial music. It's quite hard to equate Simon's urbane observations with the harsher realities of the staged commercial presentation.

Yet he has masses of experience. Educated at Balliol. President of the Oxford Union. Nine years as a TV interviewer in New Zealand. Director of European Public Affairs at public relations company Hill & Knowlton for six years. A Partner at Brunswick. A key player in John Major's private office. Director of Communications at British Airways for several years, and now in one of the country's most sensitive jobs.

He immediately agrees about the vital importance of chemistry in any presentation.

66 **You know whether you're in with a chance within the first two or three minutes ... but just sometimes you're saying to yourself 'God, this is dull', when someone says something which just grabs your attention.** 99

He says he hates technical support, screens and PowerPoint and that it somehow

66 **puts my mind in the wrong place – worrying about the technique, not the message.** 99

(Intriguingly he observes that PowerPoint is enthusiastically used at Buckingham Palace.)

But this doesn't mean he's against visual aids *per se*. He recalls great presentations where walls were filled with charts and where flipcharts have been used to brilliant effect.

At a pitch to the Angolan government when he was at Hill & Knowlton he had to simplify the presentation.

66They all spoke English, but only up to a point. Speaking more slowly was essential, as was the need to use words with Latin rather than Anglo-Saxon roots. 'Keen' became 'enthusiastic' in a late redraft.99

He makes the point about the 'well thought-out conversation'.

We pause as I observe how apt a summation this is – the strong and comforting smell of Mansion polish fills my nostrils as I glance around his wonderful room.

the essence of conversation is
interplay and interruption and anecdote

Simon is a strong proponent of the power of storytelling – philosophy doesn't work on most people. He also espouses the 'less is more' approach.

66As a victim of countless presentations, I have been amazed how many people exceeded the brief and, on the basis of very little knowledge, have tried to tell me how to run my business when all I wanted was some brilliant PR.99

The most potent presentations contain the sense that the presenter knows more than he's telling:

66Little flashes from someone with a whole pocket of knowledge.99

Simon told me about the worst ever presentation, well two actually. One, a personal experience, being asked, 'right, where's the presentation then?' when he'd been briefed to have an informal chat. Interestingly this was from a firm of management consultants (they've never been noted for their own communication skills).

The second was in New York. In historic loyalty to an old employer, Simon got Hill & Knowlton on the British Airways pitch list.

66 **We arrived to be greeted by these 18-year-old girls with little hats on and short skirts ... they were Bunny Girls but why, I wondered, would they decide to get Bunny Girls to greet us and then hand us packets of peanuts with 'Hill & Knowlton and BA – the Makings of a Great Partnership' on them?**

I suddenly realized they were meant to be air hostesses.

We went into the presentation room and, well, it was unbelievable, they strapped us in our seats.

It went downhill after that.

All the other agencies had presented executives who, if they hadn't chosen PR, could have credibly been in a bank or a law firm. We were presented to by old guys who looked like they'd been out drinking with journos. 99

As regards the best presenters in the communcations business, Simon gives a clear list of three. In reverse order they are:

No.3 Philip Gould (New Labour's master of spin)

No.2 Alan Parker (founder of Brunswick Public Relations)

No.1 Tim Bell (founder of Chime Communications and former MD of Saatchi and Saatchi).

But he also gives an important and clear caveat.

66 **There really isn't such a thing as a brilliant presenter ... there are brilliant presenters to specific audiences.** 99

Chemistry is king. If you don't like Tim Bell, no matter how hard he tries you still won't like him (as he's quick to admit himself).

And I once saw Philip Gould come a cropper (what is it with New Labour and women?) at the Women's Advertising Club of London. Wendy Braverman in her vote of thanks for a powerful, fascinating but – clearly to his audience who liked him no more than he manifestly liked them – uneven performance, said:

66 **I'm often asked why so many people take an instant dislike to Philip Gould.**

I always say, 'well, because it saves so much time' 99

Ouch.

So advice to would be presenters.

1. *Never over-run*. Simon tells the story of a top PR executive speaking for 55 minutes instead of 25 and then passing a 'hurry up' note to his flustered successor.

2. *Play the team*. 'A nerd can work brilliantly if he's a specialist part of the team.'

3. *Don't score points*. Simon remembers how hard it was for John Major, Norman Fowler and, particularly, Brian Malwhinney to perform together without appearing in competition during the election run-up.

4. *Invite (and get) open forum.*

He ends by quoting from US TV presenter Ed Murrow, who said (not his exact words):

66 **In this TV age the two most disastrous presidential candidates would probably have been Lincoln and Jefferson who had, respectively, great ugliness and a squeaky effeminate voice.**

The model candidate would have been Warren Harding who looked like a Roman senator but was also the worst president. 99

Which only goes to show, presentation isn't everything.

part four

THE WORLD OF PRESENTATIONS

  chapter sixteen
  The Tower of Babel 251

  chapter seventeen
  Welcome to presentation city 258

OH MY AMERICA, MY NEW FOUND LAND
(or why we find american presentations sexy) 261
  Interviews with master presenters
      John Triggle, Charles Rosner – *HTRP*
      Nigel Clare   – *formerly of Heinz*
      Teresa Ceballos   – *Heinz*
      Marc Wolff   – *pilot*

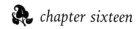 *chapter sixteen*

THE TOWER OF BABEL

Presenting to multinational audiences

To most of us presenting is challenging enough without having to communicate to a multinational audience, some of whom have a shaky grasp of English. The possibilities of people getting the wrong end of the stick – or of getting no stick at all – seem rich in potential.

Yet this may be where the real art of presentation merely comes into its own. Even if we're presenting in English to English people, the real impact of our verbal communication comprises only about 15 per cent of the impact we deliver. So let's start with the 'performance' part of the presentation.

It happened to me.

In the Martinez. In Cannes.

It was an international advertising conference with an audience of English, Americans (so far so good), French, Germans, Portuguese, Italians and Spaniards. The English language was in somewhat short supply.

The English language was in somewhat short supply.

The brief was frighteningly simple: 'Just show them some of the ads you've done, tell them a bit about the agency, how it's doing, and what the strategy for the future is.'

The night before I had nightmares of Andrew Sachs-type characters (like Manuel in *Fawlty Towers*) uttering puzzled '*que*'s?' as I struggled to do this.

I decided to act out of character. My creative director dressed smartly (or as smartly as creative people can) in a suit, shirt, tie and polished brogues. I, on the other hand, forsaking years of besuited anonymity, dressed in black trousers, black shirt (no tie), had rumpled hair, and I do believe I actually wore dark glasses.

The audience eyed the creative director suspiciously (well, he did look like an accountant), but surprisingly they took to me (perhaps the Italians thought I was mafioso).

The first thing I did was throw away my script. If they weren't going to understand it, my following it slavishly seemed pretty futile.

So I walked around a lot and tried to establish some common ground.

The more animated I became, the happier they seemed. Good learning this. Body language – give or take the odd gesture – is well understood by nearly everyone. And I used words they probably felt happy with, such as 'advertising, business, clients, awards' (boy, they really understood that) and proper names.

A sister agency, WCRS, had a brilliant, famous, maverick chairman – Robin Wight – who was larger than life. I found just mentioning his name got a laugh. Unsurprisingly, I found myself mentioning it a lot.

I eyeballed them a lot (easy to do behind dark glasses), showed them commercials and communicated three things:

- We're doing well.
- We love this business.
- We like being here with you.

And it worked. They even seemed to enjoy a commercial which had proved incomprehensible to the housewives of Middle England.

By then, of course, we were in a state of group euphoria.

At the end a Spaniard who spoke good English came up to me and said: 'That was wonderful … so creative … I just wish I could speak English like you.'

For once in my life my body had worked harder than my mouth and my ears were listening to my audience, not to myself.

So it needn't perhaps be that hard. Just force yourself to communicate very simple, very tangible things. Philosophy goes out of the window.

And it honestly doesn't matter if you get it a bit wrong.

When John F. Kennedy said in West Berlin in June 1963: '*Ich bin ein Berliner*' (which apparently translates as 'I am a doughnut'), many found it hilarious, but most paid tribute to the bravura of an American President trying to communicate to his audience.

The multinational audience presents you with the rare challenges of being very simple and connecting with them.

I once heard a non-English-speaking Frenchman address such an audience. As I recall, he said something like:

'*Bonjour* ... (very long pause) ... *bonjour mes enfants ... bonjour mes amis ... je vous adore... salutations mes amis ... vous êtes* (he struggled mightily, peered at his notes in bemusement and said) ... the greatest'.

We applauded wildly.

We felt motivated.

We thought he was great.

And that it was a damned fine presentation.

Language need not be a barrier. Regard it instead as a springboard (and not in itself the most important one) to aid real audience communication. It's not what you *say*.

It's what you *mean* that matters.

And for those who have to do more complex presentations, remember:

- Facts speak louder than words.
- Specifics beat generalities.
- Simple numbers are understood by everyone.

But don't try this one at home. English-speaking audiences take it amiss if you start performing like Jacques Tati in *Monsieur Hulot's Holiday*.

Presenting at international conferences generally, however, poses problems. The British are particularly uneasy in such environments. You suddenly realize English may be a common language and the words people use may look like English, sound like English ... but they don't mean what we think they mean.

A colleague tells of a Singaporean he met at a conference who, although he spoke perfect English, took the somewhat individual view that if his slides said what he wanted to say there was no point in speaking to them. Perhaps someone had told him not to read the slides. Anyway, he went through slide by slide pointing at them, offering them, smiling to his audience, but saying not a word.

Working abroad

Standards around the world have improved greatly in the past few years and London and New York are no longer the sole centres of excellence.

Yet the language barriers and the technical barriers remain a problem. You need people with local knowledge who speak your language in order to get things done fast and efficiently. When the wrong video appears at your conference it is helpful, to say the least, to have someone who can interpret the string of expletives correctly and take the appropriate action.

And language barriers exist as ever between the US and the UK. For a recent conference in Berlin an American client insisted on a 'switcher'. The production company queried this, but the client insisted – and was appalled when he arrived to find that a simple unit for switching between sources awaited him. A switcher. He expected what Europeans call a vision mixer, and it took several hours of panic, and an overnight flight, to rectify the problem.

Technical problems are slowly reducing and the solutions becoming automated. But in the US in particular there is less than widespread knowledge of international technical standards and great care should be taken, with videos especially. Most still think that PAL is some sort of friend.

The problems of culture and technology, especially when compounded by a foreign language, can also produce unexpected problems.

It was the second day of a long, elaborate conference for a Japanese company. The speeches and slides were all impressive, the equipment top-notch – great sound systems, high-tech slides, videos, autocues – the whole bit. The British presenters, although they said it themselves, were pretty impressive. Enter Yoshi, the Japanese MD, about to go on stage. He looked dreadful. White. Shaking. Exhausted.

He looked dreadful. White. Shaking. Exhausted.

66Yoshi, are you all right? You look terribly tired.

Up all night. No sleep. Learning presentation. Word perfect. You guys learn yours by heart. I have to do same.

But Yoshi, we used autocue.

Autocue? What's autocue?**99**

Translations

English bullet points are heavily dependent on context for their meaning and can often be honed down to very few words without altogether losing it. This is not true in many other languages and translation of minimalist presentations from English is fraught with difficulty.

English into German tends to produce much longer words, and into French many more words; both will play havoc with your layouts.

And an innocuous phrase such as 'Record sales' can legitimately be translated as either *'Ventes énormes'* or *'Ventes de disques'*.

If you don't speak the language well enough to judge for yourself, beware! Presentational English is full of such traps.

Simultaneous translation

We were working for a Russian oil company. Not a dull experience. During the first presentation we had arranged simultaneous translation, which was fine.

Not a dull experience.

However, the Russian love of long and impressive speeches meant that this short, snappy presentation took nearly an hour. A very, very long hour. So it was decided to halve the presentation for the lunchtime meeting and it was cut rigorously.

Only the translation at lunchtime was sequential – the Russian CEO spoke a sentence in Russian, then the translator gave it in English. So back to an hour again …

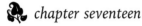 *chapter seventeen*

Welcome to

Presentation City

Global presentations in today's world

I t's 7.30am.

The car park is already half full.

Marketing executives are squinting at their computer screens.

The quiet buzz of success fills the air.

This is H.J. Heinz at Hayes Park, near Heathrow.

This is Presentation City.

Why are presentations so important to Heinz employees?

66It's part of the culture.

It's a necessary mechanic – a kind of intellectual paper trail. It makes you focus on what you're trying to achieve.

I feel I've got somewhere when I've done the presentation.99

So it's HQ's way of imposing control and it's subsidiaries' way of proving their mettle.

And what's more, presentations are addictive.

66One year we spent nearly six months preparing the annual plan. It was terrific. A work of art. People in Pittsburgh said they'd never seen anything like it. We got rave reviews. They still talk about it.99

When I asked if those six months could have been more usefully spent talking to customers or to consumers, the first reaction was, understandably, defensive. But as time passed a sense of reality prevailed.

66We just played the game and, bear in mind this is competitive, people make judgements on how you say it, not just what you say.99

But nearly everyone agreed the business priorities were out of kilter, that

worrying more about what you say to your peers than to your market is seriously daft

Well actually, the brain agreed but the instinct – that corporate nerve that will carry on working when all executives everywhere are brain-dead – reached out to produce yet another PowerPoint presentation. It's impossible to kick this presentation drug. Once you're on it, you're hooked. People are trained to watch presentations and behave in presentation mode – polite but interested (you score points for the validity of your interruptions, especially if you spot something like an arithmetical error). People spend their days presenting to each other. This is corporate life. This is Presentation City.

Well, it was.

But it's changing. New senior executives have now gone gung ho for content not presentation.

The worldwide CEO wants his presentations in ten slides, not 50. The trouble is, the 50-chart executive is reduced to tears by this new edict in abbreviation.

❝I can't get it all in. It's like the bloody Emperor of Austria – 'too many notes Mozart'. How can I tell the story in ten slides?**❞**

While the more enlightened cut through the presentation morass.

Just talk. Tell the story without props and slides.

(Yes, like many, he's read Rolf Jensen's *The Dream Society* and its espousal of storytelling in presentations.)

Now to those who use decks of slides as an alternative to a story – what we'd call the telephone directory school of fiction – being asked to appear on a naked stage without the camouflage of a presentation is pretty frightening.

As Steven Spielberg said, speechmaking is frightening, and it appears that for some the rules are changing.

OH MY AMERICA, MY NEW FOUND LAND

(or why we find American presentations sexy)

part four

🍎

Interviews with master presenters

God Bless America

🍎

The American Dream

John Triggle, A Senior Partner, HTRP; Charles Rosner – Public Sector Solutions

🍎

Thinking faster than you can speak

Nigel Clare, former CEO, Heinz Retail Europe

🍎

Presenting through the glass ceiling

Teresa Ceballos, Manager, HJ Heinz

🍎

But is it good box office?

Marc Wolff, leading film helicopter pilot

🍎

God Bless America

It really does depend on who you talk to as to whether Americans are seen as great or lousy presenters. My own view is close to that I have about American literature. The greatest, crispest writing comes from across the Atlantic and has done for some time. Who can forget the transforming moment of first reading *Catcher in the Rye*, *Catch 22* or *Bonfire of the Vanities*? Who can doubt *Barbarians at the Gate* is one of the most powerful stories about a corporation ever told?

The greatest, crispest writing comes from across the Atlantic

But not, it appears, for many Englishmen. These comments came from interviews with a number of British businessmen:

- 'The Americans are low on empathy.'
- 'They're very process orientated and very conformist.'
- 'They *need* to present and do so at any opportunity (look at IBM in the Eighties – a complete presentation culture).'
- 'They lack sincerity.'
- 'They live in a praise culture. They meet their kid at the school gate and say "Hey Josh, good waiting, kid", or play golf with their wife who scuffs the ball 20 yards and say "Hey, it's getting there, sweetie", not "Crap shot".'
- 'They talk within their comfort zone.'

It's all a little like a Monty Python sketch, and what did the Americans ever do for us?

So why such hostility?

Basically, we conclude, because the British are a hostile race. Hostile, argumentative, aggressive (that's what Americans say in riposte). Scenes that we regard as commonplace in the House of Commons would be totally unsuitable in Congress.

Quite simply, Americans play the game – present to the corporate format and are comfortable in so doing. In contrast, we in the UK are always trying to get out of the box.

> ## Americans play the game – present to the corporate format and are comfortable in so doing.

It's the Worldcom Conference in Florida 2000, Disneyland. As one of the bonding sessions groups go on an imagineering course. They are asked:

What do you see?

(It's 80°F. It's by the side of the pool. I see bare-ish bums and lots of suntan oil.)

The Americans:

66 I see heaven – angels playing guitars, Mr Jiffy, the ice cream man, playing leapfrog with Jesus. 99

The British:

When's lunch?

As the session developed, a game of Consequences was devised. The Americans took part eagerly and imaginatively (it was, after all, an imagineering course). The storyline was handed from person to person until it reached Liz.

66 **Liz, tell us... what happens next?** 99

Fed up with the whole thing, Liz told them:

66 **And it all went dark.** 99

There was a silence.

66 **Is that all?**
Yep. It all went dark. 99

Yet this puzzling denigration of American presenters expressed by many British and European presenters will certainly irritate Americans who have variously confided in me their own dismay at the arrogance of their British counterparts.

66 **You represent 10 per cent of our world sales. Well done. But that doesn't entitle you to claim the majority voice in being right.** 99

Interestingly, David Abbott, of whose prose we have spoken, learned his craft working for Doyle Dane in Madison Avenue. To those who know him there is a secret that must at last be revealed.

David wrote in American.

Pause by his open-doored office as he wrote an ad and you heard this American voice speaking. David reading his copy out loud.

Why? Because he found it a more direct, pleasing language than stuffy, obfuscated old English, that's why.

And the Americans have such wonderful confections in their phrasing.

Static/declining sales	=	**Flat growth**
Loss	=	**Negative profit**

❝In this new global economy maybe it's time we took a leaf out of Bananarama's book (almost) and started speaking not Italian but American.❞

We also believe the difference between American and British presentations is diminishing. The impact of management gurus, business schools and management books, and the growing trend towards business globalization, is having its inevitable effect.

Most British presenters are discovering a new voice. One that is more powerful, less tendentious. Arguably the communications centre of the world is nearer Hollywood than Chorley Wood. And so what is changing is the language of persuasion – more 'hear this' than 'excuse me'.

From a personal viewpoint I see this as a good thing. It's a joy to speak the language of 'let's go get 'em'.

But it is not the first language of the British. In America, whatever the ins and outs of their education system, the confidence of public speaking is drilled into people at an early age. The average American comes from the school of Clint Eastwood, with a perfect comprehension of acting small and communicating minimalistically. Our presenters (until recently) have come from a long line of Henry Irvings (the stage as opposed to the silver screen).

American presenters to a man and woman proclaim themselves 'comfortable in their shoes' presenting. All that we can teach them is to be a little more culturally flexible and to remember that American football is an arcane sport to Europeans.

remember that American football is an arcane sport to Europeans

And it's sad that the worst American presenters today are nearly always politicians (come back Ronald Reagan, all is forgiven).

The Glossary of Management Speak from Pussyfoot to Powerfoot

English	American
Good morning.	Hi!
I've got one or two slides.	Here's the deck.
I just wanted to mention.	Now listen to this.
Our results are not unsatisfactory.	These figures are great.
It would be remiss not to mention.	Thank you stars. Stand up Ed, Bill and Lucy. Let's hear it for them guys.
Competitive pressure continues to be intense.	Look guys, we're bleeding and we've got to fight back.
Our new product looks promising.	It's going to kill those suckers in Cleveland.
It's pretty clear.	It's a no brainer.
Thank you for listening.	You are a wonderful bunch. I'm proud to be here.

I recently saw Al Pacino's documentary on *Richard III*. It was full of remarkable insights on the play (the most performed of all Shakespeare's plays – yes, even more than *Hamlet*). Equally it's full of the British/American divide on language and performance.

Michael Williams, the late actor, described it perfectly.

❝The Americans are made to feel frightened of Shakespeare, of interpreting him and performing him ... he is ours not theirs.❞

But as Pacino said of Shakespeare:

> 66It doesn't matter if you don't understand every word… do you ever understand every word of anything?… it's whether you *get* it.99

I was electrified.

Here was American intelligence interpreting a complex play and making it work because brutal intuition, not academic genius is what is necessary in understanding things that matter.

> ## brutal intuition, not academic genius is what is necessary in understanding things that matter

This division of culture, it occurred to me as I watched enthralled, is claptrap. Good for a cheap laugh on our part. Good for a smart remark on theirs. Bizarre to reflect that the sounds Richard of Gloucester actually made were far closer to Pacino's utterances than they ever were to Laurence Olivier's since Shakespearean cadences apparently sounded quite American.

Yet the most important point was not this but that given great content with complexity of meaning and subplots to baffle a Poirot, the American performer pushes further, pushes deeper to unravel what's really, really going on.

> ## the American performer pushes further, pushes deeper to unravel what's really, really going on

Al Pacino is no average performer. He's no average performer because when he uses his mind he's awesome.

This documentary taught me two things.

1. Performing ability and thinking ability aren't and shouldn't be separated.

2. The process of production of any performance or presentation should be in the planning phase:

- ruthless
- confrontational
- interrogative
- questioning everything
- aiming for the most real, convincing performance.

It taught me something else I already knew. The Americans on song have balls of steel (that's also what Dianne Thompson of Camelot was said to have in a *Sunday Times* interview, to her huge amusement). They also have minds of steel – when they use them.

It occurs to me that their so-called presentational shortfall lies in often not having to be as active and self-questioning as they always should be.

The next time they present in the UK and Europe they will, if they've read this book, be dynamite.

You see it's easy. Give a talented American a great script and they're capable of flying to extraordinary heights.

Al Pacino. You just won my Oscar for Presentations.

John Triggle, Charles Rosner
The American Dream

John Triggle, one-time CEO of Spalding Worldwide, and Charles Rosner, founder of Public Sector Solutions, sat opposite me. They looked ready to go.

> 66 **I love presentations.**
> **I can tell people things they need to know.**
> **I love selling … it's so much fun.** 99

The American Dream.

Selling. Telling. Storytellers one and all. Anecdotes spill from their lips. The best, the worst presentations.

I ask them to set the scene for me. John Triggle, a former county squash player, expat now domiciled in New York and a Senior Partner of the consulting firm HTRP, reflects.

> 66 **It's a changed world now. More media driven. Animation. High tech. Everyone's presenting to everyone and doing so with a lot more polish than ever before.** 99

Charlie, a tennis ace in his early life (they called him First Round Rosner – not good enough to go any further), flicks a bit of dust from the cuff of his immaculate Brooks Brothers suit. He is a presentation in himself without uttering a word, but when he does utter, does he utter.

> 66 **The cost to most organisations of making the top man look good in presentations is escalating fast. It's becoming a big but hidden budget item.** 99

Charlie used to run courses on how to present at Lord Geller, once a great New York advertising agency, mainly to the hundred or so creatives there.

He taught three things:

1. Know when you've won.

2. Know what to do when you've won.

3. Know what not to talk about.

Short answers (must have been a very quick course but very instructive):

1. If they say 'can I see the ad more closely' and if the clients actually touch and hold it, well, that's a very, very good sign. It means they're owning it.

   And if they say; 'Gee you know what we could do with this?' it means they've bought it because it has legs and *they* can not only own it but use it.

2. Go.

   Get up.

   Say 'thank you' and leave.

   Do not allow any possibility of unselling the ad.

3. Never talk about the ads.

   Show the ads.

   And talk about *their* business.

An art director who says, 'When I saw the brief I thought about the trade marketing problems you must have being the third brand in the market' makes the clients much more likely to love his wonderful visuals than the one who says, 'I wanted a visual integrity'.

John reflects on identifying the decision maker.

Jean Amic, a suave Frenchman at a leading French fragrance oil manufacturer and now on the main board of pharmaceuticals company Hoffman La Roche, led a huge team to Estee Lauder in New York to present a new fragrance range.

There it was. The GM building. The Estee Lauder senior executives, eight or nine of them. Powerful men and one short (4 foot 11 inches) lady, greying slightly, unobtrusive – a secretary perhaps?

The trial began. Sniff. Sniff. The air filled with exotic language about 'distinctive notes, the undertone of vanilla, the dying embers of mint, the full blush of peach, round, flat, full, burgeoning, dramatic …' Wine tasters eat your hearts out.

The moment of decision. Five voted for number one. Definite choice. No doubt. Three voted for number two.

Jean Amic turned to the little lady. 'And Mrs Lauder (for Estee Lauder herself it was), what do you think?'

Unblinkingly she said: 'Number four.'

'Number four? Why is that?'

'Because, young man, it smells of money.'

Identify the real decision maker. It saves so much time.

His second story reinforces Charlie's about when you've sold it get up and go and don't unsell the already sold.

A meeting with Leonard Bernstein. His flat. Two senior executives from a major Hollywood studio – no Mickey Mouse operation – and the maestro with attendant advisers.

Agenda: To persuade Mr Bernstein to adapt his already existing *West Side Story* score for an animated film version starring cats.

Great presentation. Great meeting. Sold.

As they left, the shorter of the Hollywood executives (so short indeed they say that 'when he stood up his head didn't move') leaned forward, patted Leonard Bernstein's arm, and said: 'And Leonard, please can we have a happy ending?'

The maestro frowned: 'Oh fuck it, do you think that Shakespeare got it wrong too?'

The film never happened.

Get out when you're ahead.

Charlie Rosner reflects on surprises. Unsurprisingly, he hates them. 'They are death to selling' (remember, this is American speak). But he adds with unexpected emotion: 'Remember Shakespeare and his prologues. He told you the godamned plot in the first 60 seconds or so. No surprises in great theatre, none in presentations. It's a rule.'

'Just remember,' he continues 'three things *fix* every presentation (if only we could always remember to do it):

1. This is what I'm going to tell you.

2. This is what I'm telling you.

3. This is what I told you.

Dress it up how you like (you're going to write a book on this – you must be mad), it's as simple as that.'

The rules are simple.

● Always run things by people first.

● Never enter a battle you're going to lose.

● Identify each person's agenda when you present to them.

('If you give them what they want, they *may* give you what you want.')

I've always been impressed by how flexible Americans are. The land of ephemeral enthusiasms – 'I gave up being a vegetarian years ago', 'Oh that idea, I ditched it last week but have you heard my new one?' Like the Weebles, the Americans may wobble but they don't fall down.

George Lois. The legendary New York art director. The man who stood on a 20th-storey window ledge threatening to throw himself to his death unless a client bought an ad. George the Giant and the dramatist presenting to a client.

GL: 'This is not only the best (dramatic pause, adjustment of shirt collar and up with the vocal volume), this is the ONLY conceivable advertising campaign you can run.'

Client: 'But George, we ran a campaign like that two years ago. It failed miserably.'

GL: 'Right. Right ... I'll be back Tuesday.'

And out flounces George.

And a trick on how to sell the one you want.

It's very simple. Mount it on board just 5 per cent bigger than all the rest. Amazingly, this works.

And to conclude, not from America but from Italy. The father of the current Duke of Bedford was designing a villa in Rome. Five designers on, one after the other. The consecutive, competitive pitch (chorus line by another name – 'Next ...').

Our man (I really think he must have been American) went on last. 'Where,' asked the Duke, 'are your drawings? Everyone else had plans and stuff.'

Our man took out a sketchpad. 'I wanted to know how you saw it ...'

He embroiled the Duke in a debate about what could go where as he drafted expertly and slowly away. 'The conservatory here perhaps ...'

As time passed he subtly and expertly rubbished his predecessors, involved his client, and gave him ownership of the project.

JOHN TRIGGLE, CHARLES ROSNER

Unsurprisingly, the Duke gave him ownership of a large amount of money when he awarded him the contract.

The American Dream made real – winning by listening, by learning and by thinking on your feet.

Nigel Clare
Thinking faster than you can speak

My mobile phone rings. It's 6.30am. I answer wearily. 'Hi, it's Nigel ... ' brightly on the other end of the phone. Early birds and worms, that kind of thing. Another day, another performance, Nigel Clare is presenting again.

When I started this book with Martin, Nigel was Managing Director of Heinz Grocery Europe. By the time we went to proof stage he'd been promoted to CEO, Heinz Retail Europe, responsible for sales of $2 billion. By the time we went to print he'd left Heinz for new challenges (the theme of speed in corporate life is consistent). Nigel is an intellectual and a real street fighter, a magic combination which emanates electric energy. Living proof that you don't have to be a bastard to win and that nice people have teeth.

He has only one rule for presenting.

Connect and care about connecting with the audience – or don't bother!

We talk about the great connectors:

Winston Churchill – 'So much, so many, so few ...'
Martin Luther King – 'I have a dream ...'
Bob Hope – 'There's nothing I wouldn't do for Bing and nothing he wouldn't do for me. And that's the way we go through life – doing nothing for each other.'

❝One wonderful Brit, a wonderful American and one wonderful mix of the two.❞

They all connected.

They all made people believe and laugh. They all changed minds, behaviour and moods.

Nigel talked about all of them as timeless icons. 'They are all compelling and they connect. They gladden the heart and they change the mind.'

He says thinking of these help him connect when presenting. And he has a few dos and don'ts. 'Not tips for God's sake, I do it more from the gut than the intellect. These are my intuitive check points.'

1. Learn to think faster than you speak (some of us can write faster than we can think so this is a tall order).

2. Connect with your audience.

3. Care for culture. Understand it. Use it.

4. Be creative. Surprise people. Make it simple to understand.

5. Play to the overlap ('I don't want to give you X or Y ... I want to give you A then B then X and then Y').

6. Play with and use audience expectation.

7. It's good to be nervous – it shows you care.

Nigel stops speaking and stares into the middle distance. He's thinking (it's like watching your computer monitor on one of its thoughtful days) and when that thinking takes time he exploits the devastating silence to commanding effect. He says eventually he is always looking for that 'hey listen to this' sound bite.

Rather like the late, great libel lawyer George Carman on former Tory MP Neil Hamilton:

66 **a man on the take ... and a man on the make.** 99

He enthuses about lines like that that work. Enthusiasm is probably his middle name – Nigel E. Clare.

❝There is a different language in presenting. More verbs, more numbers, fewer adjectives. The trouble with politicians is they speak written, not spoken, English.❞

And yes, there are two different languages. 'One communicates at, the other communicates with.'

I encourage him to reflect, as a senior figure in a major US company, on the differences between British and American presentations. Unsurprisingly, his view is broader and more philosophical than some others are.

❝To understand this you have to understand the American culture – their spirit of adventure, their predisposition to go off into the great unknown, their joy in delivering something new.❞

He describes the American gene pool as containing a huge dose of exploration and a belief in the probability of rags to riches being there for the taking. Britain, to be sure, is multicultural, but not new, one or two generation multicultural, like America.

The collision of cultures and the spirit of hope set against the enormity of the country – a place where 'big is beautiful' – creates a uniquely exciting recipe.

❝This is probably the smartest economy we've ever seen.❞

It has enormous power and an enormous sense of push. Most of all it has the ability to move on fast to new opportunities.

In contrast, Britain is a problem orientated society, happier at Dunkirk than Armistice Day, a society where mending what's broken motivates more people than creating what's unthought of does.

NIGEL CLARE

66 Don't get me wrong, Britain is enormously inventive and very clever. It's probably true that we are more resourceful at getting out of scrapes than any other culture. We have strong intuitions and are very creative, but the Americans are just faster. They very often start off with the answer. They ask more questions and bigger questions. 99

This distinction between the tactically driven, syllogistic British and the strategic, 'beam me up Scotty', take-me-to-the-destination Americans manifests itself in presentations.

The Americans are happy at flying a kite, doing agenda-setting presentations, while the British are not.

66 Britain is more of a blame culture and the most extraordinary aspect of this is the damnation that falls on the most successful.

The Americans love a winner for ever. The British love a winner for a moment. 99

On success in adversity:

66 Richard Noble (the guy who designed the vehicle that broke the land speed record and the speed of sound) set up a web site to get the public to pay for fuel for the final record attempt. A great speaker, inspirational and peculiarly British – everything done on a shoestring. 99

Nigel is an accomplished presenter who enjoys it not just on a functional but on a creative level.

66 The moment when you throw something at an audience and you sense something happening ... it's a chemistry ... it's almost palpable ... the sense of minds changing. 99

He also adores pressure and believes pressure can make presentations work:

Too much time and they get floppy.

And links this to the old adage:

66 Necessity is the mother of invention. 99

because they have to be.

The most creative presentations are those that are produced up against the wire.

I wonder if this is true.

Is the 'mother of invention' different in different cultures? Necessity in the UK maybe, philosophy in France, clarity in Germany, ouzo in Greece, mañana in Spain, and in America:

66 That next challenge, the new horizon ... I don't know, maybe. 99

But then he reflects on Apollo 13 and how the necessity of finding a life-saving solution in just one-and-a-half hours concentrated the astronauts' inventive minds wonderfully.

Nigel never stops presenting. He uses his mind, enthusiasm and energy to communicate his presence centre stage. He slides from topic to topic in a frenzied intellectual gavotte. It's exhilarating stuff, but then again we have the comfort of knowing:

He's thinking faster than he's speaking.

Not the only person mentioned in this interview to have broken the speed of sound then.

Teresa Ceballos
Presenting through the glass ceiling

Teresa Ceballos works for Heinz. She is Global Category Manager on Quick Serve Meals and manager of the biggest quality standards initiative any food company has ever embarked upon. She has worked for Danone in Paris, Scott Paper in Paris, Kimberley Clark in the USA. Her parents are deeply educated Spaniards, originally from Madrid. She was educated in Washington, has a degree in Business and Art History from Georgetown, and has an International MBA from Thunderbird, Phoenix, Arizona.

A real international star. Bright, funny and focused.

She is not on the board of Heinz (not by a long chalk yet). She is not a CEO. But she will be, she will be. As an inveterate talent-spotter I know these things. And she loves presenting.

66 **Because I'm a natural ham ... I love creating dialogues with groups of people in a more interesting way.** 99

And she knows she's good at it (she is, by the way).

66 **They're good, my presentations, because I have empathy with my audiences. I worry about four things:**

- **who they are;**
- **why they're there;**
- **how they feel (their mood and expectations);**
- **what I can do to entertain them.** 99

She confesses to one flaw which springs out of this.

TERESA CEBALLOS

66 Sometimes I get too excited because I do enjoy the process so much. I speak too fast and I overuse humour, which can demean you. Trying to please your audience too much is probably a fault. 99

She has a uniquely international experience of presenting being trilingual (French, Spanish, English) and counterpoints the presentational characteristics of each.

The Americans

● They're the best coached at presenting.

● It starts at school where public speaking is a big thing.

● Presentational nuances are common:
  —hand gestures
  —the pregnant pause
  —dramatic body language
  —moving away from the podium
  —directly addressing the audience, 'Hi Bob, well, how do you feel about this?'

● She calls all this 'dialoguing' with the audience.

● Sometimes too well rehearsed, it becomes fake.

● To many American businessmen presentation is a key to corporate life.

The Spanish

● Naturally ebullient, passionate and full of dramatic gesture.

● Forced into corporatist presentations in English they commonly become:
  —stern
  —solemn
  —stilted.

- Eloquence turns to caution.
- Joy of life becomes soured.

The French

- They establish logic platforms – facts, not intuition, rule.
- So they don't mind presenting in any language – they're always the same.
- They're philosophers, not showmen.
- They belong to the Descartian school of presenting.

The English

- Variable:
  —from a plank of wood to
  —a natural comedian to
  —Churchillian inspiration.
- Humour is very important to the English presenter.
- As is irony (tricky stuff irony – doesn't travel well).
- Self-deprecating, often without the power words which sprinkle US presentations.

Teresa sees the Americans as the world-class presenters but with all the formulae which, misapplied, can lead to communications disaster.

Her particular horror story is of CEO acting out the role of football coach.

❝Guys. Here's the story. Here's what's up.

You know we've been losing share and the downsizing has led to quality issues. You know we've had problems.

So what we gonna do? You gotta help me out here.

So let's win it for the Gipper.

OK? 99

Message: 'We're all in the same boat.'

Response: 'Oh no we're not' – and – 'let me out of here.'

CEOs and their employees are simply not at the same level and it is gauche to think they are.

Teresa's worst presentational experiences are all at conferences (or in church) where the presenter (sorry, padre) is presenting without an audience pre-brief and where dialogue is reduced to monologue.

Her best are always audience focused, with evangelical fervour and which tell you something relevant and interesting. And that fervour and passion is, she believes, key.

66How you give information nowadays is almost as important as what you say. 99

She is a strong supporter of visual aids but with the emphasis on visual.

66Pictures create impact. It's great to talk to pictures. They bring words to life. 99

Teresa learned her presentational skills in the American Deep South – Birmingham, Alabama. She has huge but not unself-critical self-confidence and she understands the biology game.

66A pretty woman is generally more pleasing a presenter than a troll. 99

But she also sees how presentations equalize and so, if you're a good presenter as a woman, you can crack the glass ceiling.

if you're a good presenter as a woman, you can crack the glass ceiling

She observes shrewdly that successful business is a 'moderation game' and that from a woman's perspective it's important to be:

- not too conservative
- and not too slinky
- not too bitchy
- and not too nice.

(Sorry Teresa, you've probably failed here. Much too nice.)

But she ends with powerful advice to men and women alike, French, Spanish, American or British.

66 **If you're passionate about what you say, it works. And presentations are a great forum to get *your* point of view across.**

But most of all, have fun.

There's not enough fun in business and probably too many presentations. 99

Marc Wolff
But is it good box office?

Marc Wolff is a Vietnam vet. He flew helicopters in the Mekong Delta and spent much of the late sixties being shot at. Now he does something much more dangerous. He works in the film business. Marc is acknowledged as the world's leading film helicopter pilot and has credits on hundreds of films, including the James Bond classics, *Superman*, *Star Wars* and many others.

Presentations mean little to him because it isn't his stock in trade, not in so many words.

He pitches ideas. Sells ideas for film stunts. Listens to others describing a particular move or storyline.

In other words he lives through presentations on a daily basis, creates, debates storyboards (presentations?) and so on.

He said two things that intrigued me.

66 Everyone, whoever they are, has a commercial failure – be it Robert Redford, Kim Basinger, Brad Pitt ... 99

So it is with presenters, however good they are.

Secondly, he counterpoints, without denigrating either, the performances of Robert Redford and Brad Pitt on the recent *Spy Game* shoot.

66 Robert Redford was word perfect, step perfect, movement identical on every single take ... take 18 was the same as take 1.

Brad Pitt was, candidly, variable. No two takes were quite the same. But god does the camera love that boy. 66

And how can anyone possibly say to any presenter 'make sure the camera or, in your case, the audience, loves you?' but, as with a

Hollywood star, do not eschew those things that help make this curious chemistry happen:

- how you look;
- what you wear;
- how you move;
- how you speak;
- your reputation (if you were lousy presenting the last two times out it won't much help).

Business has an increasingly deep hunger for presenters.

Hollywood has an insatiable appetite for movie stars.
Just remember Tony Carlisle's advice:

"Never, ever make a presentation that doesn't matter."

Or, as Marc put it:

"Avoid crap films if you can."

part five

Conclusions, Confusions
and Curtain Calls

🔖 *chapter eighteen*
   And finally …   291

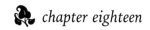 *chapter eighteen*

AND FINALLY ...

I have this macabre vision of someone who has just finished reading this book and is about to do a presentation. A little like a golfer who's just read *That Perfect Swing* and is standing on the first tee waiting to transfer his weight, come inside to out, release his right hip and, for God's sake, not forgetting to pronate his wrists. Does any golfer, in passing, know what pronation means? It sounds painful.

Anyway, there you are. You've prepared with intense care. Your children avoid you because they're bored with your practising on them. Your spouse is walking about with a dazed expression – neither of you have slept for days as your rehearsing keeps you both awake.

Your slides are by now so cryptic they are positively sinister.

Sales up in the third quarter by 40 per cent

now simply says

Up!

Positive signs of market growth

now says

Yes! Yes! Yes!

and

Radical structural change

says

New.

You've had a new haircut and had the grey bits dyed. Your younger daughter says you look like a cross between a punk and a member of the Mafia. You have a new light grey suit.

And the night before in the hotel you rehearsed finally and nakedly in front of a full-length mirror. It was unfortunate that you'd left the 'Make My Room Up' card on the door. The chambermaid who came in ran down the corridor screaming on seeing you dramatically saying 'and do I have something special for you' as you stared manically into the mirror. The hotel was very nice about it really.

You allow yourself a certain nervousness on the morning, a certain adrenalin lift, but you realize this means you are so hyped you are speaking to everyone very, very fast.

'Goo mornin Jo lovely day innit? Gosh you look well an ows yourwife?' you say to your boss as you pass him.

'Have you been drinking?' he asks suspiciously.

It's time to go on stage.

Then, like Jim Prideaux in John Le Carré's *Tinker, Tailor, Soldier, Spy*, who remarked that under interrogation it's only the things you've hidden deep and want to conceal that you can actually remember, you can only recall the horror stories, the 'don't dos' other experts mentioned.

So you go into Presentation Mode. You dramatically enter in a hunched form, limping slightly (you banged your knee backstage). For all the world you are Richard III.

You jangle your change. You turn your back to the audience. You read the slides (hard to do when they only say things like 'Up' or 'New' or 'Yes' but you do it nonetheless).

Then something goes wrong with the mike. It doesn't actually, it's just that you keep remembering to get out from behind that lectern and walk about and, as a result, the sound engineer has a problem. Just as he turns the volume up in desperation so that the audience can catch what you're saying, you lunge for the mike and bellow into it:

'So are we on the verge of breakthrough?'

Deafened, the audience gasp. A girl in the third row starts to cry. You remember the need to be interactive.

'Hey Jill, remember the good times we had in this company?'

She is now crying and blushing.

You employ the devastating silence.

1 – 2 – 3 – 4 – 5 – 6 – 7 – 8 – 9 – 10 – 11 –

12 – 13 – 14 – 15 – 16 – 17 – 18 – 19 – 20.

You have your audience transfixed. They stare at you, occasionally throwing embarrassed glances at Jill.

'Passion,' you recall 'not had enough of it yet.

Because *I* remember the good times ...'

Jill is led out in hysterics.

You tell a joke. No one laughs.

You praise the stewardship of the managing director.

Everyone howls with laughter (they've only just got your joke).

You know you're over-running and you know this is bad. Something in your brain throws the 'abort' switch and you finish somewhat surprisingly in mid-sentence.

'And so ... and so ...

Thank you.'

You leave to confused applause because, yes, in its own way this has been a sensation.

There is no magic bullet in presenting. But amid all the advice, the hints and the anecdotes, a few key messages burn through.

There is no magic bullet in presenting.

1. *Presentations are increasingly important.* They are a great way of getting important messages across to people. And you and your career prospects will increasingly be determined by how you present.

2. *Presentation isn't just about standing up there and socking it to them.* It's about how you set the thing up, how you manage expectations of what it is and why it's happening. It's about what you do afterwards to follow up what's been said. It's about how you look, how you dress, how you behave.

3. *Substance vanquishes style.* Something strange happens to people when the word 'presentation' is mentioned. A tendency to think in presentation mode. Everything goes into chart form. The demon 'jargon' suddenly comes into his own.

   Yet we know that if we know what we are talking about, just getting up and telling it like it is can be effective.

   > So before you do anything else, make sure you have a good solid story to tell.

4. *Tell me a story* ... with a beginning and a middle and an end. The dramatic, narrative drive is what most often will make a presentation sensational. Storytelling runs deep in our souls. We like them. We understand the format.

   But do remember one thing. The short story is the most difficult one of all to tell.

5. *Audiences need to have their attention grabbed.* There's so much going on nowadays – what John Perriss, former CEO of Zenith called a 'cacophony of sound'.

   When all is said and done they don't have to listen to you. In their heads they are listening already to all sorts of other things. To their spouse grumbling about how hard they work. To the opening passage of their own presentation which they are about to give.

You must make them hear what you are saying.

Don't be dull.
Don't be complex.

Tell them what you're going to say, say it, then remind them what you've said.

6. *Preparation is all.* Some need more preparation than others just as some actors learn their parts faster than others.

   But everyone, repeat everyone, needs to prepare.

   Give yourself time. Do lots of drafts. Hone them. Be like Bill Clinton. Able to present when the presentation itself is wrenched from your grasp.

7. *Conviction is convincing.* Passion, we keep on hearing, is key. It is.

The passionate belief in the story you are telling can be enormously seductive.

There's too little of the stuff in the world. Too much cynicism. Too much pessimism.

Make sure your presentational glass is always half full and never half empty.

8. *See it from their point of view.* Spend at least as much time thinking about the audience as you think about yourself. What do they know? What do they think? Why are they there?

Is the reason they're there different from the one they believe? What do they expect, need, want from you? How far (if at all) are you trying to change their minds?

See it from their point of view if you want them to see it from yours.

9. *Redundancy*. What anyone who does an unnecessary presentation deserves.

If you haven't got anything to say, don't say it. And if you have, have the courtesy to say it as well as you can.

10. *Enjoy it*.

How? Performing in public is torture for some.

There are a few obvious bits of advice.

- Make sure you're comfortable in the environment, with things as you want them.
- Make sure you feel good – your dress, your mood, etc.
- Don't be too ambitious (avoid over-complex technology).
- Don't allow any surprises to occur and if they do, have a backup plan.
- Convince yourself you are powerfully in charge of the agenda.
- Go for it.
- Oh, and smile from time to time.

Something shows consistently in all our master presenters' comments and that is that they are:

- very interested in people – how they *react*, how they *feel*;
- more interested in *what* they are talking about than *how* they talk about it.

It's curiously hard to find your own voice, but you can and you will. Telling an actor to 'act naturally' is about as intimidating a stage direction as anyone can imagine. And we are not exactly saying 'act naturally'. We are saying find that voice, that mode of address, of attire, of body language with which you feel comfortable.

It's about seeking out those sensations before the event that you recognize as signalling the prelude to your being a Presentation Sensation. **Good luck.**